RANDY FOX

THE CALL to EXCELLENCE

INFLUENTIAL LEADERSHIP FOR IMPACTFUL RESULTS

The Call to Excellence

The images used at the beginning of each chapter include pictures from Freepik. Learn more at www.freepik.com.

The Call to Excellence: Influential Leadership for Impactful Results

ISBN: 978-0-9914669-7-9

First Printing, 2024

Printed in the United States of America

Interior Layout: Trevor Fox, messengermedia.solutions

Cover Design: Eli Creasy, elicreasy6.wixsite.com/ecreasy

TABLE OF CONTENTS

THE WORKBOOK

Welcome, friend! Before we jump into this amazing journey, I want to make you aware of two resources that are available to you. First is the FREE Workbook, which I've put together to help you get the most out of this book.

You can utilize the workbook as you wish, yet my recommendation is to read a single chapter in the book, pause, and complete the corresponding section in the workbook before continuing to read. Each section contains an opportunity for reflection and a call to action.

To download the workbook, scan this QR code:

A deeper dive:

For a more full, transformational experience, additional inspiration, and a "coffee table" type conversation; check out my companion video course. This resource is the perfect opportunity to discover behind the scenes thoughts and hear more powerful stories.

There is an approximately 10 minute video for each chapter, totaling nearly 2 hours of exclusive content.

Scan this QR code to learn more:

Now on to excellence!

OPENING THOUGHTS

Silver Platter Service (the book and keynote) has been touching hearts, improving teams and changing our culture for the last half a dozen years. The imagery of the platter is the reminder to serve, to grow, and a harkening call that beckons us to excellence.

We start today where that book finished off, with a brief excerpt of the story that inspired the silver platter service movement.

When it's time to collect the trash on an airplane, the typical experience we have is that the flight attendants open up a big, plastic trash bag and walk down the aisle.

You hear them say, "Trash, trash, trash."

They literally look right at you and call you trash!

To be fair, this process does the job, the bag collects the trash.

It is adequate, and it is efficient.

We expect this.

We accept this.

What we don't do is rave about it. We aren't moved by it. It does nothing to provide us with an experience of excellence.

Abraham is a flight attendant I met in 2017, and he served the passengers with such excellence.

He comes out of the galley, still in full suit, no apron, no gloves, no trash bag.

As he approaches the first row to collect their trash, he surprises us all with an empty, shiny, silver platter!

After he has completed the trash collection in row one, he walks back to the galley, empties the platter, and returns to row two. Again, with a shiny silver platter.

He repeats this process, and comes back again, to each row, collecting trash with the silver platter.

He gets to our row, and are you ready for this?

He politely asks me, "Sir, are you done?"

"I am," I said.

"May I take this?" he asks.

"Yes, you may," I reply.

And his response, "You're too kind."

I was too kind to give him my trash on a silver platter!

My friends, this is excellence with just a small, seemingly meaningless task of collecting trash. Imagine the excellence you will bring to your life and those around you if you provided this type of service!

You can serve others in this manner. There are a myriad of tasks, projects, or responsibilities that with a slight tweak can become excellent!

> The Call to Excellence *is the opportunity, responsibility and honor before you to influence people and impact results in the highest manner.*

What will you do to create these types of moments for your team, your client, your family, and your community?

When I say "The world is waiting for you," this is what I'm talking about.

The world is starving for this type of love and servant leadership that delivers excellence.

Certainly the silver platter lives on, yet it's time for us to take it a step further.

Higher.

Next level.

A new gold standard.

Excellence!

The Call to Excellence is the opportunity, responsibility and honor before you to influence people and impact results in the highest manner.

Let's GO!

PREFACE

★★★★★

It was a typical weekend night at my childhood home. My mom, brother and I were in the family room watching TV, eating a cheese and sausage pizza from Gina's. I so miss good Chicago-style pizza.

The home phone rings.

We had two phones in the house, one in my mom's bedroom in the far end of our ranch home, the other phone was a landline rotary phone located in the kitchen. The kitchen phone was about 25 steps (or 8 long leaps) from the couch I was laying on.

That ring brought my brother and I quickly to our feet and the race was on!

We jumped up and ran to be the first one to the kitchen. First one there gets to answer the call.

We felt like such adults getting to answer the phone, and not knowing who would be on the other end was part of the excitement.

Would it be a friend asking to play? Maybe it would be Uncle Jim inviting us over. Or maybe it would be our grandpa, calling to check in and stay connected to his daughter and grandsons.

"Fox Residence," I would say, as I always got there first. Well, I should have, I'm six years older than my brother, Steve.

This time it was one of my mom's friends. That was boring. "Mom, it's for you." I would set down the corded phone on the kitchen table and slumber back to the couch in the other room.

Growing up in the 70's and 80's was a far different time than it is today, yet some things are still the same.

One of the things that hasn't changed is that people desire to remain connected, in a variety of ways. And the calls are still made, and through them, we pursue life in the most excellent way.

Or at least we should.

When the phone calls are made today, the knowledge of who is calling is revealed as their name pops up on your device, and yet, the joy of someone reaching out remains.

It's always exciting to get the call.

Other times in life, though, you get to make the call. And that can be just as exhilarating. Reaching out to connect with someone special can be a time of laughter and love.

I remember a vivid time of making the call on our family vacation road trips.

My grandpa would help prepare us for the trip. He and I would go to the local AAA office to get a printed map of the route, and while we were there, he would share a few important details and expectations of me.

He was concerned with his now divorced daughter, and her two sons out on their own. So much so, he would get his car all tuned up, oil changed, gas tank full and hand my mom the keys to his brand new Oldsmobile.

That was the call he made to help his family.

Upon arriving at our destination, he wanted us to call him as soon as we walked in the door. I believe it was in part because he wanted to know we arrived, yet I also think it was because he wanted to know his car wasn't in a wreck!

We always called him using a toll number and asked the operator to charge it to him. The calls were special, yet short, because they were so expensive.

The call is something we are all familiar with when it

comes to phones and devices and speaking to others.

How about all the other types of calls you make, accept (or don't) in your life, though?

You've had key decisions, key moments, key opportunities that shaped your journey, and those around you.

With the concept of the call, this book is about making them, accepting them, and living them in your life. We will take a journey together of a completely different type of call.

It's the most important call. This is the call of your life!

The call that sometimes is made or accepted, yet always one that needs to be lived out with excellence.

This call is not transactional, irrelevant or flippant. This call is the core of your being.

It's the ongoing call to make a difference.

The call to embrace moments, accept a mission and live life to the fullest.

The call to start, stop, move, influence, change, innovate, befriend and love people and life. This isn't about barely getting through, or surviving, or just getting by.

This call is about thriving in all aspects, personally and professionally. It's about making a profound difference in the world and all those you influence.

No more status quo.
No more average work.
No more good enough
just being good enough.

This is the call of your life!

This isn't about being perfect, though either. It isn't about having all of the answers. It isn't about how much power, money or material possessions you have. Nope, none of those.

This is about living life, doing work, building relationships, all with a single pursuit.

Excellence.

It is time, my friend.

Come with me as we explore the possibilities, joy and fullness of a life lived well.

A life that truly changes the world.

It's time to maximize your potential, increase your performance, and be truly fulfilled in your life.

You may be asking, "How do I do this, Randy?"

I'm so glad you asked.

Excellence.

It's time for the call to excellence!

CHAPTER ONE

What is Excellence?

Before we get too far into the conversation, there is value in us having a basic understanding of excellence, and what we are trying to achieve in our pursuit.

Let us first clarify what excellence is not.

It's not perfect. We are not pursuing perfection. We are accepting a call to excellence.

Working, living and growing in excellence is very different from being perfect.

Perfection is when there are no flaws, no errors, and no defects at all. It's a state in which we would find no fault in any way, in anything, or with anyone.

Perfection is something that is unachievable, unattainable and unsustainable.

Too many of us live with an expectation of perfection, both of ourselves and of others.

We must alter that perspective and replace it with a pursuit of excellence. Excellence is achievable, attainable and sustainable.

This is my definition of excellence and what I'm referring to:

The highest standard for the thoughts, words, actions, and life of an individual or organization.

Excellence is not only possible, its impact is profound. Someone or something, that is excellent, changes the world.

Our world could really use some of that.

Here's the thing, though, excellence doesn't just happen. Sure, I believe in blessings and miracles, and I've experienced so many good things that came my way apart from my own effort.

However, there is much to be said for personal responsibility and the opportunity each of us has every day to pursue excellence.

The pursuit of excellence is realistic and so much more impactful (and fun) than the pursuit of perfection.

When the pursuit of excellence is done consistently as an individual, and then collectively as a team, the results will be amazing!

So, what's the pursuit of excellence?

Here's my take on this most noble pursuit in life:

The pursuit of excellence is a continuous quest to improve one's thoughts, words and actions, so the impacts are at the highest and best possible level.

If the concept of excellence is new to you this may sound very lofty. Maybe even intimidating.

Stay with me here.

Status quo just won't get it done.

Good enough isn't good enough.

The standard needs to, and must be, higher.

This is a quest for the best, the highest, the most excellent in all of life.

The pursuit of excellence
is a continuous quest
to improve one's thoughts,
words and actions,
so the impacts
are at the highest and
best possible level.

This is a quest for those wanting to walk the path less chosen. It's a walk that will maximize your performance, increase your results, and most importantly, bring you joy and fulfillment in your life.

Want some of that?

Oh, I'm glad you do and I'm glad you're here, it's gonna be a great ride! Let's continue our quest.

Connection Point Church is led by my good friend and pastor, Jerry Roames. My wife Marne and I actually founded and launched the church with Jerry and his wife, Lori, sitting at our dining table five years ago.

Even though our world is drastically different post-pandemic, and we are in a different church building than we started, a few things in our church have not changed.

God has not changed, nor His Word, and neither have our values. Our church has four core values that are the pillars of who we are.

One of the values is to *pursue excellence in all things*.

We are constantly looking to be our best, give our best and expect the best from others.

We are on this great noble pursuit, and we do so as a team.

We are always making sure that what we do is excellent. This ranges from the welcome people experience when they pull in the parking lot, to the cleanliness of the bathrooms, to our kid's area volunteers, worship experience, donut wall (yes, we have a donut wall) and on and on. You can see more at connectingme.church.

Average is unacceptable. Everyone is expected to pursue excellence in their service role.

It doesn't mean we don't make mistakes. It doesn't mean we don't miss the mark from time to time.

What it means, though, is we don't accept the misses or leave things to be stale or average. We don't make excuses and we don't accept the lack of excellence.

The journey isn't always easy, because people are involved. As you know, when people are involved, things can get messy.

However, we work to be excellent because that is what we are called to do.

One of our mantras at church is that to be excellent we must be open to feedback. We have to be willing to hear a gentle critique. To be excellent, my friend, you must be unoffendable.

Ooh, did I step on some toes there?

Yes, unoffendable.

Give some grace.

Realize you aren't perfect either.

Be open to be better.

And that brings us right into what the entire pursuit is all about. When it comes to excellence, you must always be looking to improve.

Continuously.

Vigorously.

Bravely.

Back in the early 2000's, I was a young and aspiring leader. At just 30 years of age, I was promoted to plant manager of a $35 million operation with nearly 200 employees.

As I look back, I may not have been quite ready, but I answered the call. I was all in for the responsibility to lead a team and make the necessary improvements to create a culture of excellence.

Even though I was rather young compared to my 54 plant manager colleagues in our vast corporation, I brought passion, energy, new ideas and a desire to take care of our customers; both internally and externally.

Hear me on this, I wasn't perfect, I didn't have most of the answers, and I certainly made mistakes. Saying that, though, I was hired because what had been happening under the previous leadership was not working.

Customer service was lacking. There was poor, if any, communication. On-time delivery wasn't high enough. Employees' attitudes were full of grumbling, and the list goes on. The culture wasn't excellent and they demoted the former leader to promote me.

In my first days and weeks on the job I walked around, a lot. Like most of the day. As I met people and began to get to know them, I asked questions.

When I asked someone why we did something a certain way, "Because we've always done it that way," was the most common response. I very much disliked that response.

Guess what I did when I heard that? I asked more questions.

The bottom line, my friend, is that if you don't understand why you are doing something, or if you can't explain why it's the most excellent manner in which to serve, work and live, then you need to ask more questions.

This applies to anything and everything in your life. Your work, relationships, parenting, finances, and so on.

You need to always be questioning if something is excellent and you need to be looking to proper sources to find the answers.

In my new role, I knew there would be skeptics. I knew the task was large. Yet, I also knew that with a pursuit of excellence as our focus, we would get better.

And we did.

We set all kinds of sales and profit records over the next several years. We grew our business, launched several new product offerings, and our customer service became the company benchmark. So much so, I was asked to go to other facilities and help bring the team focus of service excellence to their locations.

Now, none of this happened without changes. And none of it happened without getting everyone on board with the noble pursuit of excellence.

Fast forward several decades since that story. I have met some amazing people in my speaking career.

Recently, while traveling to an event, I had the pleasure to meet Jamie Miller, the Founder and President of JA Wastewater.

Her company specializes in helping rural and non-service areas clean water from waste. As she puts it, "They clean the water of the world one drop at a time."

This is important work for sure. We need water to be treated, clean, and safe; otherwise, people die.

Literally.

Owning her own business for decades, she pointed out her discovery on success and results. She shared with me, "Randy, in order to be our very best and deliver the highest level of excellence possible in our work and lives, we need to slow down. We need to take time to do it right the first time. The people we serve and impact deserve our very best, every time. It's just that simple."

Jamie is right.

Our fast paced, meet the deadline, too much going on to care about details, or people, mantra **has to stop**. We need to slow the pace, deliver our best, and stay on a quest for excellence.

It's easy, though, to get off course. That's why later on

we will cover the keys to remaining on your desired path by increasing margin, building lasting relationships, and focusing on the things people of excellence always do, and the things they never do.

This is going to be a great journey, and I'm grateful you've chosen to spend your time with me.

As we prepare to move on, let's wrap up what excellence is.

My life, like yours, has had many ups and downs. I've had many memories filled with pride and joy of positive impacts I made on people and organizations.

I also look back and am amazed I got through the storms, many of which I caused myself.

In my nearly 55 years on this earth, I have found there is something, and someone, that is most excellent.
A foundation that never fails, that leads the way, that sets the bar for excellence.

I have a guidebook for life and living. It's my source of truth. It's the cornerstone for excellence.

It was inspired by my great friend. It's filled with strategies, insights, wisdom and stories on how to live a life of excellence.

That book, and that friendship, is what has given me the foundation, the hope, and the encouragement to share with you how to answer the call to excellence.

> *What you do will influence people. It's up to you if that influence will have impactful results that bring you closer to others, closer to joy and closer to excellence.*

What book is it? I'm glad you asked.

The Bible. It's all about my God and friend, Jesus. I believe He has a plan for me, and for you, and that plan involves a life full of abundance. You could say, a life of excellence.

I hope the book you're reading now will help launch and sustain your journey and quest to find excellence. We will unpack how we live out this noble call by showing up, by bringing our best, by influencing others in positive ways, and by always improving for the most impactful results.

You make calls everyday.

You accept calls, or not, everyday.

You choose to live out these calls, or not, everyday.

What you do will influence people. It's up to you if that influence will have impactful results that bring you closer to others, closer to joy and closer to excellence.

The question before you now is this: Will you make, accept, and live out these calls to pursue a noble life and excellence in all things?

I'm so glad you said yes!

CHAPTER TWO

★★★★★

Courage and Commitment for What is Right

I was a basketball referee for over 30 years, which put me on the court for approximately 1,000 games. Not as many as some, yet more than most.

What still amazes me is how many calls I was involved with during that span.

An average game has 33 fouls called, plus a couple dozen violations, and nearly double that in total decisions that result in a no call. That comes out to approximately 120 calls per game, wow!

With 3 officials per game, on average, each will have about 40 calls a game. Simple math, that puts me at about 40,000 calls over the span of my career.

That, my friend, is a lot of calls. A tremendous amount of pressure and responsibility.

There are also 40,000 opportunities to be wrong, to be booed, to be disagreed with, and to be made to feel lesser than human. And trust me, that happened frequently.

One of the most memorable calls I ever made in a game also turned out to be one of the most tense moments of my career.

Two of the top teams in the conference were facing off. The home team was favored and the visitors came to win. We had a close one all game long. As legendary TV announcer Keith Jackson would say, "Oh, we got a barnburner here."

Back and forth the scoring went, so up and down the floor I went. The closer the game got to the end of regulation, the more pressure and greater the impact there was on each call. The coaches, players and fans had rising intensity in their excitement, emotions and disagreements with our calls.

With just 8 seconds to go, the home team was down by 2 points, and they had the ball. They brought it up the court quickly, passed it to a speedy player on the right wing near the bench side. She eyes up the defense and decides to drive the lane and create an opportunity.

The offense and defense are stride for stride driving down the right side of the lane, directly at me. I was positioned as the lead official on the baseline.

This is the moment when your experience shines. The moment as an official that you dream of; making the key call late in a close game. The call that literally could decide the outcome.

And this one would.

You have these moments in your life, too.

The pressure is on, and someone needs to step up and face the challenge. Someone needs to make the call. People are depending on that. People are depending on *you*.

A decision needs to be made.

Will you step up?

If not you, then who?

My friend, they are waiting for you!

The world is waiting for you!

Now, the offensive player is about 10 feet from the basket.

She quickly and briefly extended her arm and displaced the defense backwards. The offensive player's movement allowed her to have some space to stop, turn and have an easy pass to a wide open teammate at the three point line.

Tweeeeet!

That tweet was my whistle sounding to the arena that a foul occurred. My right arm went up, the arena gasped with air, and for a split second, the roar turned to silence. All eyes were on me.

What would the call be?

I literally took a two step jump hop to the left and gave my best George Foreman right jab punch. Yep, I shipped it to the other end. Offensive foul!

The home team now loses the ball and the clock shows only 2 seconds remaining in the game.

I could have held my whistle. I could have "let the players decide the game" as so many commentators and fans incorrectly say.

My friend, if something is wrong, if someone commits a foul and we don't call it, we haven't let the players decide. We decided for them it was okay to break the rules.

It isn't okay. Ever.

It isn't okay in basketball, on your team, in your organization, in your community or in your family.

The call has to be made. Right must win. Period.

We cannot have excellence with any sacrifice to the highest expectations of greatness.

To say the coach of the home team was upset is an understatement. He may not have moved that fast in his life.

"Randy! You can't make that call! That is terrible, you are terrible, I can't believe this," were just a few of the remarks he screamed with ever increasing volume.

We cannot have excellence with any sacrifice to the highest expectations of greatness.

I calmly walked with him up the sideline as I reported the foul. I listened to him for a bit and tried to explain the displacement, but he was having none of it. I kept my slow gate like I was strolling on a Saturday morning in the park.

Once I passed half court, I turned and gave a visible stop sign with my hand, and firmly stated, "Coach, that's enough, that's your warning."

He continued to act like a child who didn't get their way. I'm sorry, but there is no other way to explain it.

I wish I could tell you I made one more call, because I should have. He deserved a technical foul. I'll get back to that in a moment.

The game was now decided as the opposing player made her 2 free throws. The home team would get the ball back, but they would lose the game.

And the coach would then absolutely lose his cool, too.

As I, and my officiating crew, walked off the court to the tunnel that led to the official's locker room, he must have turned into a bull and mistaken me for a matador. This 6'5", 250 pound angry coach comes charging at me.

He was cursing, yelling, spitting and was as close to me as he could be without touching me.

I thought of stopping. I didn't.

I thought of responding. I didn't do that either.

I simply kept walking.

He was physically restrained by several people and we finally made it safely to our locker room.

I have to admit, as I sat down, my heart did race a bit. My emotions were high, and it took some time to unpack what just happened.

Back to me not giving a technical. I knew at that moment the game was over. I didn't want to add insult that late in the game. The reality is, though, it was the wrong call.

Not sure if giving a technical foul would have changed his behavior after the game, yet it would have sent a message in the moment for him to stop. It would have demonstrated that the behavior was beyond unacceptable and that I was calling him on it.

After the game, the three of us officials called our boss, the coordinator of officials, from the locker room to discuss what just occurred. He had actually been watching our game online, so he already knew what happened.

He supported us, also wished a technical had been given, and was already working on his statements to the commissioner of the conference, and the athletic director of the college.

Remember, not making the right call when something is wrong is wrong. The conference officials and the school were wrong. They did nothing about the situation.

Nothing.

I spoke to my coordinator about a week later. I was extremely disappointed to hear they were condoning that poor behavior. I found their lack of expecting, demanding and holding people accountable to a level of excellence to be unacceptable.

After working Division III basketball for 20 years, including in that conference and a trip to the Final Four, I retired. I gave notice I would no longer work at that level.

Instead of officiating, I stepped into leadership roles and became a coordinator of officials myself. I wasn't giving up, I wanted to have more influence.

Friend, the world needs people to step up and address the wrongs that occur. We need people to continually pursue excellence in all things. We must hold one another accountable. And above all, how we treat one another as human beings needs to be at the top of the list.

We need to respect, honor, care and love one another.

We need to be there when others need us, even when they

may not realize we were needed.

What call do you need to make today?

What call will you make that leaves the world in a better place?

There may be only a few seconds remaining, the game is on the line...and this is your moment.

Go ahead.

Be brave. Be bold. Lead well.

It's time to make the call!

CHAPTER THREE

Where Does Your Compass Point?

One of my favorite movies of all time, is actually a whole series of movies. *The Pirates of the Caribbean* takes us on a journey of swashbuckling humor, action and victory in some of the most obscure ways.

The acting is great, the music is amazing and the movies, of course, remind us of the fun and exhilarating ride found at Disney World.

The worst pirate you've ever heard of, Captain Jack Sparrow, is played by Johnny Depp. In typical Depp fashion, Jack is crazy, wild and constantly drawing your eyes and ears to his every word and action.

The Captain occasionally commandeers a ship, grabs the wheel, asks for the horizon and looks at his compass for direction. The perfect fit for this off balance captain is that he has a compass that doesn't work.

That's right, it doesn't point north. He's following the guidance of something of absolutely no use at all; something broken.

A compass is a resource to help us with our direction to ensure we are heading to the destination and location desired.

Your life at work, home and otherwise is heading somewhere. All roads lead somewhere.

The reality, though, is that if you don't have a working compass, or other navigational system, you may very well find yourself arriving at a point you do not desire. And once you get lost, it may be too late.

You need to know you are headed in the right direction. A direction that brings you desirable results and outcomes.

A working compass will get you pointed in the right direction. In today's modern world, we use navigational systems known as GPS.

Your GPS system matters, so let's break down a proven system for directional success.

GPS

G is for Guardrails.

Last winter, my family took a trip into the Smoky Mountains. The views while driving across the mountain range were breathtaking. So much so, I got distracted from driving while taking in God's creative masterpiece.

Living most of my life in Illinois, and now in Florida, flat is the land of most of my daily views. But, there's something special about that rugged mountainside, the rising peaks and the clouds floating around the tops and diving into the valleys.

It's absolutely beautiful.

As we drove along the twists and turns, I was amazed by the engineering concepts and execution. I also wondered, how, so many years ago, they cut through the terrain, built the roads and sometimes bore through land to create tunnels to drive through the mountain!

As we drove to higher elevations, we had some very tight turns, and the car literally felt like we were about to fall off the side of the cliff. If it weren't for the guardrails they put up, many vehicles would have done just that.

You can tell by the long dark marks left by metal hitting metal.

That guardrail isn't placed off the mountain edge. It's actually placed several feet away from the cliff's edge, enough room to keep a swerved vehicle from crashing down.

The guardrail protects from injury and accident, and, for the most part, keeps the passengers safe.

The same is true in your life.

You need guardrails.

One of my friends has a specific guardrail that I find unique in the world. I also know it works.

Decades ago, he made a promise to himself and his wife that he would not be alone with another woman.

Never.

He would not ride in a car alone, go out for dinner alone, and certainly not meet alone behind closed doors.

If something at work requires him to meet with a woman, he either invites another person or has the meeting and leaves the door open.

Now, I'm not saying he doesn't have self control, I know him well, he does.

What I am saying is that just because you know how to drive a car, doesn't mean something can't happen, you swerve, and without the guardrail, you are off the cliff.

This is why my friend has the guardrail. He doesn't want to get close to falling. The risks and costs are simply too high.

Guardrails help you avoid situations that lead to actions, behaviors and outcomes you don't desire.

What types of guardrails do you need in your life? How about at work?

Financial budgets and reports are a type of guardrail. Do you have them? Do you follow them?

Do you have people, situations or places you need to stay away from?

Guardrails help you avoid situations that lead to actions, behaviors and outcomes you don't desire.

Do you need to limit the amount of time you spend on social media, tv, or video games?

What do you need to put in place to better guide you to your desired destination and outcome?

Don't wait until it's too late.

Guardrails, good for drivin', good for livin'.

P is for Principles.

I shared some of this story in my book *A Leader Worth Following*, yet wanted to take a different approach and hit some other key elements.

In 2005, I met up with a couple of guys who were investing in real estate.

They asked me to find them renters, who would eventually become buyers. They offered them a 2 year lease with predetermined pricing to buy the property. I made a nice commission for each renter I brought them.

The opportunities came fast. It sure seemed like this would work well.

Imagine having hundreds (even thousands) of dollars of cash flow every month and then tens of thousands of dollars on payday once they buy? Now, multiply that by twenty, thirty or even one hundred properties.

I was so fired up about creating passive income and getting out of the daily grind. I thought, "Why go to a job everyday if I can just have money come to me?"

I just had to get in the action.

Prior to the passing of my first wife, she advised me not to invest in this. She believed it was too risky. She didn't see this as something I would enjoy. She was fully against the endeavor.

You would think that after being together nearly 20 years, I would listen to my wife.

Nope. I pressed on.

My uncle, one of my most trusted advisors growing up, advised me not to go into the venture.

Nonetheless, I pressed on.

Early in 2006, I purchased two properties and placed two tenants in the homes. I had financial freedom!

Or so I thought.

Less than two years later a major recession hit. The housing market crashed and my properties were worth about 10% of what I purchased them for.

That isn't a typo.

TEN PERCENT.

My tenants couldn't afford the rent, no one wanted to rent, and I was forced to cut their rent by 50% just to have some revenue coming in. It wasn't enough though, we now had more money going out than coming in.

It was awful.

Repairs. Unpaid water bills by tenants. More repairs. Tenants not paying rent at all.

This was the opposite of what I had dreamed of.

I wanted out, big time, and now! But there wasn't a good way out.

Several more years passed. The bills climbed, as well as the frustration. It was just a mess.

In reality, unless I was willing to give up 90% of my investment, I only had two choices. Short sale or hold on. The bank would consider a short sale, but told me that they would basically decimate my credit rating.

I spoke to family and friends, trying to figure out what to do.

The two guys that I had started this endeavor with had bailed. One got out just before the crash, the other filed bankruptcy.

I was on my own.

At about this time, my lead pastor asked me if I would preach one Sunday on leadership. I was just starting my speaking business and this would be a great opportunity to get some platform experience.

As I did research in the Bible on leadership, I came across a verse from Psalm 15:4. Psalm 15 speaks to who can rise up and be worthy, and verse 4 says, "He who keeps an oath even when it hurts."

This was my "Aha" moment! My heart and head came together and I figured out what I was supposed to do with the real estate.

Keep my oath.

I signed a mortgage note. I promised to pay it back. I was responsible for this. Period.

Just because something is legal doesn't make it right. There is no integrity in going back on our word.

There is a lack of character and honesty when we bend for

our benefit and sacrifice what is right for personal gain. This puts cracks in our foundation.

This isn't being a person with principle.

The world will tell you to do what is best for you, to use the law to your advantage, and as long as it doesn't hurt anyone, it's ok.

Well, I'm here to say, it's not ok.

Never.

Your GPS goes off course when you sacrifice your principles.

Prior to 2009, I used my feelings, emotions and needs as my guide.

Since then, as I previously mentioned, I have a guidebook, the Bible. It's full of everything needed for life and living.

So, back to my oath, which I kept through all the hurt.

Years later I finally sold both properties. I lost money on them both. But, I honored my principles, and God honored me for that.

I still have good credit.

I was always able to pay every single invoice for the nearly 18 years I had the two homes. Always.

No loans, no credit cards, the money was always there.

But this isn't just about the money. My heart was changed for the better.

I know I messed up. I learned a lot about real estate, about business, about myself, and what I was supposed to be focused on.

Instead of chasing money and not trying to work at all, I discovered that doing work that matters brings us greater rewards.

Stand firm in your principles. Your GPS works so much better when you do, and you will stay on your desired course.

S is for Sincerity (truth).

The phone at the desk of a seasoned sales executive rings. "Hello, how may I help?" Jeanne was always ready to serve.

"Jeanne, this is Doug with ABC retailer." (name and company changed)

"How are you doing, Doug? It's so great to hear from you!"

Jeanne is excited as she hasn't heard from Doug, a great client, in several months.

Doug had contracted the company Jeanne worked for to provide a new technology solution. It was a leading solution using personalized URLs combined with actual loyalty gifts for consumers of the brand. This was brand new in the marketplace and Doug loved the work, the service and the team Jeanne represented.

"Well, Jeanne, I've been better, and I'm hoping you can help. We have gone through the invoice your company sent us for the work from this past month and it appears we were overbilled by about $5,000."

Jeanne was very apologetic, quickly ended the call and came to get the author of the contract terms and one of the key strategists for the company offering the solution, *me*.

Sure enough, Doug was correct. We had indeed, mistakenly, overbilled the client.

Ouch!

As we dug through the customer service invoice spreadsheets and compared them to the contract terms, our team had made an error in the computation formulas.

This error had, unfortunately, been occurring for more than

the past month. It had been occurring for more than the past year. In fact, our discovery was rather shocking, we had incorrectly billed the client for the past 18 months totalling more than $75,000 in overbilling.

Double ouch!!

Over the span of time, we had closed not one, but two fiscal years. For those not familiar with that term, it's like your year end tax return. The company closes the financial books, has them audited and reports the final numbers.

We were now overlapping multiple years of reporting, and, worse yet, had mistakenly and unknowingly, overbilled one of our very best clients.

Triple ouch!!!

A meeting was quickly formed with Jeanne, our senior vice president of sales, the customer service representative, our chief financial officer (CFO), and me.

The conversation started by someone stating we should simply offer to give them a credit for the month in question. "This was the only month they asked about, let's acknowledge they were correct and give them the single month credit."

Another commented, "But what about the other months,

do we just ignore them?"

And another came in with, "We can't possibly reveal that we have overbilled for 18 months, and that we didn't even know we were doing it. They will lose all faith in us, and have zero trust in our capability."

The CFO was also concerned about the integrity of the books, as they would be incorrect for two consecutive fiscal years. All of this was not sitting well.

Finally, a wise leader spoke up. This leader was calm, had their compass working and was thinking about the most important element, sincerity.

Sincerity equals truth.

"I understand the financial pain this causes, the unexpected outflow of cash, and how we don't look as competent as we would like. However, that doesn't matter. What matters is what will happen when they find out we knew about the 18 months and didn't do anything about it. Our integrity, being totally truthful and sincere is what matters. Don't give them a credit, issue them a full refund and send them a check."

Bam! That's having a working GPS.

Being sincere is about living, speaking and acknowledging

the full truth. Partial truth isn't truth; it's partially true, which means it's also partially not true.

Would you like to guess what happened when they received the call about the refund and the overbilling of 18 months?

They were thankful. They appreciated our honesty. It actually built trust and created a stronger relationship.

Fear.

Pride.

Looking incompetent.

Being afraid of what to say, or what they will say.

Partial truth isn't truth; it's partially true, which means it's also partially not true.

These are some of the types of emotions that spurred the initial thinking.

Those emotions, those crazy thoughts are like Jack Sparrow and a broken compass. You literally go round and round, driving yourself mad, accomplishing nothing.

When you are in a position where there is a fork in the road, the decision is easy. Choose the narrow path of truth and sincerity.

This path leads to trust, to a destination of healthy relationships, and ultimately, to excellence.

GPS.

Guardrails. Principles. Sincerity.

You can drive to amazing places you have never been.

You can navigate the most challenging situations in life, even ones you've never faced before, and do so with excellence.

How's your GPS working?

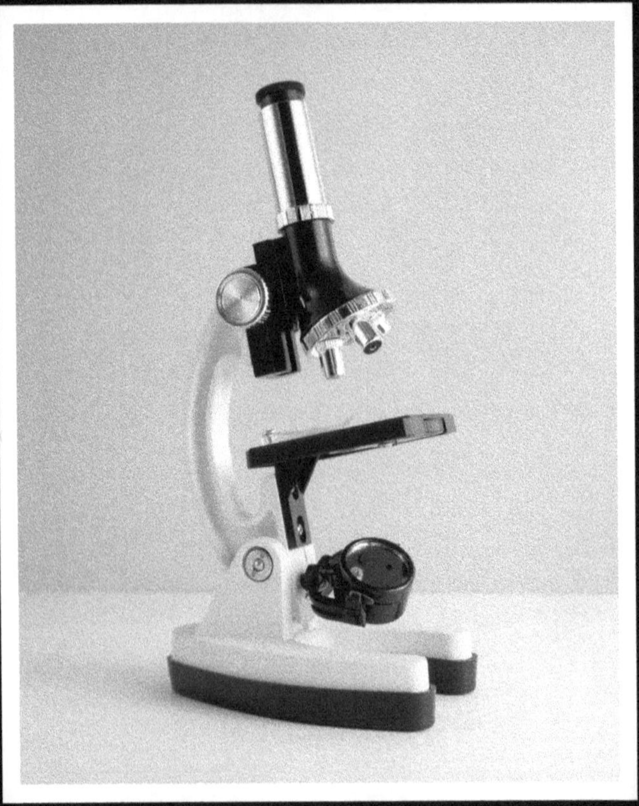

CHAPTER FOUR

The Details Matter

One time, at ~~band~~ basketball referee camp, the director was holding a session talking about the importance of details in the business of officiating. She was speaking to the things we do off the court and how to be successful.

She emphatically stated, "The little things won't hurt you, they'll kill you."

Probably a bit extreme, yet, there is truth behind it. The details do matter.

To be excellent in anything, we must be careful to take care of all of those little things.

As a strategic visionary, my natural strength is not in the details.

Certainly, though, I know the details matter.

That is why I'm thankful for my second wife, Marne. (I was blessed to marry once again). She is absolutely fantastic with details. She helps balance me in our marriage, my business, and my life. She continues to remind me of some of those things I tend to forget.

You know, like putting my dirty clothes in the proper basket.

Details do matter.

Case in point.

It's fall of 1988, the beginning of my second year in college. You could find me in room 634 at Whitten Hall on the campus of Illinois State University.

One day, after class, I walk into our dorm room and my roommate, Jeff, just kinda looks at me like we have a problem. And oh did we ever.

The wall near the window was no longer white. It had turned a rather speckled color of black, mostly due to the thousands of bugs making our room their new home.

He pointed to the hole in the screen where the infestation commenced.

There were far too many to swat, smush or in any way handle without professional help. So, off to the store we went.

Jeff had a 1980 yellow station wagon. If you're too young to know what that is, just look it up. It was cool, trust me.

We called it the banana. So clever, right?

The banana was our means of transportation, so we hopped in for a ride to the store.

We found the aisle with all the insect killing options. I picked up a can of Raid spray. It said it kills bugs dead, I was done.

Jeff wasn't impressed.

He believed it would be difficult to use the spray and ensure we get them all. He was looking at some other options that might be even better.

I kept looking too.

Not really finding anything other than different brands promising the same, I hear Jeff exuberantly exclaim, "I got it!"

I asked, "What is it?"

"Let's go," Jeff states, "this will do it."

We head to the checkout line, pay for our insect annihilation device and head back to our room.

Upon entering our room we find the situation is even worse.

More bugs!

First things first, we needed to close the window.

We were smart, huh?

Jeff believed this would be simple and handed me the box to get it done. I gave the outside of the box a quick glance and discovered the 4 steps:

1. Open box
2. Light fuse
3. Leave room
4. Return in 3 hours to dead bugs

No problem...we did just that.

We walked across the street to Avantis. For those who aren't familiar, best bread, sauce and Gondola sandwiches in central Illinois!

We ordered a loaf of bread, Italian marinara sauce and a pitcher of rootbeer.

We just sat, laughed, and talked with our friends (as many of them worked there or were in there). We hung out for about 4 hours, wanting to really make sure those bugs were dead.

Now with our bellies full we walk back and enter the lobby to our building.

We didn't make it in three steps, and we heard a bunch of people yelling in our direction, "There they are!"

We turned and looked behind us expecting that call to be for some celebrity, or worse, maybe a criminal.

Nope.

It was for us!

"What did you guys do?"

"What were you thinking?"

Those were some of the many loud and frustrated remarks that were delivered to us. Most of the choice phrases were not family friendly, if you get my drift.

The clueless looks on our faces must have given away that we didn't know what they were so angry about.

"You guys smoked out the entire floor!"

And he was serious; so were the 50 other guys relegated to the lobby.

Jeff and I took the elevator to floor six to check this out first hand. The elevator opened and we walked into a cloud.

Still nearly 4 hours after we set off this box of destruction, our entire floor was filled with smoke.

Oh my!

We laughed like jolly St. Nick on Christmas Eve.

I know we shouldn't have, but as Chris Berman would say, "C'mon, man!"

That was funny.

To say the bugs were dead is a vast understatement. We killed every microorganism and bacteria on that floor.

On the bright side, it was probably the cleanest the dorm had been in 20 years!

Hours later, when it was safe to return, we entered our room and found the remains from the box we set off.

I also found the instructions, warnings and other fine print. You know, the ones we didn't read.

If we had read the details in advance of purchasing this atomic bomb, we would have discovered some interesting facts.

This particular box was a bug bomb intended for a 2,000 square foot house. Remember, we are in a dorm, you know, like 85 square feet.

It also said the smoke could harm people if inhaled. Well, we didn't do a good job of letting anyone know this smoke screen was headed their way. Meaning, we didn't tell anyone.

As I said, details matter.

All these years later, we can still laugh about our ineptness and lack of attention to detail.

The reality, though, is that someone could have really been hurt.

This situation is a reminder to us all, our lack of attention to detail in situations can really create havoc for us, and others too.

We don't want to be slow or ineffective in our work, but at the same time, we must take a moment to ensure all of the details are addressed.

Here are 5 simple ways to make sure you don't set off a bomb that evacuates all those you care for:

1. Slow down. Truth be told, this one is hard for me. I love moving quickly and getting things done. You need to take your time and not rush too quickly to avoid mistakes and critical errors. Efficient and effective isn't rushed and irresponsible. Take your time to do it correctly the first time.

2. Get the right people involved. As I state over and over in my book *Game Plan: How The Best Teams WIN*, you are always better together than on your own. Don't try to be a solo hero; involve others that can assist, protect and provide insights that you don't see. The best results happen when you enlist help from those with proper knowledge and experience.

3. Ask the tough questions. If no one is asking the tough questions, you need to. The best leaders ask questions and listen for responses. The most excellent leaders keep asking questions. Dig for answers, and make sure

everyone around you feels safe and empowered to ask questions too.

4. Communicate well. No surprises, no gotcha moments. Everyone needs to be informed, prepared, and aware of the vision, the plan, and their role in making it happen. It's truly impossible to over communicate. We will cover more on this in the next chapter.

> *We don't want to be slow or ineffective in our work, but at the same time, we must take a moment to ensure all of the details are addressed.*

5. Have the proper solution. Just because a solution was good to solve a prior problem doesn't mean it's the best one for your current situation. You need to find the most excellent solution for each situation.

Simply put, pay attention to the details and learn from me, the details do matter.

CHAPTER FIVE

★★★★★

It's So Simple

I've enjoyed many men's breakfast meetings over the years. Sometimes there were 10 of us, sometimes just me and one other guy.

We may lead different lives, yet we desire to lead them with excellence. We held firm that iron sharpens iron. Men coming together to share the celebrations and struggles of life, building one another up, and enjoying some "guy time" is a good and necessary thing.

It has proven to me for years that it's a great foundation to have: sharing life with other people.

Recently, I was at one such breakfast with my friend Justin. He and I were discussing the challenges of entrepreneurship, being a husband, fatherhood and serving our community. What we know for sure is that life isn't easy and we don't have it all figured out.

Thus, the reason we get together.

He brought up some advice that he had received many years ago from one of his mentors. He said that it applied in all areas of life and that anyone could do it.

I was certainly intrigued.

As he shared the strategy, I was struck by the wisdom, the vastness, yet at the same time the simpleness.

Are you ready? Here it is:

"Be brilliant in the basics."

Simple, huh?

And not easy.

The basics are very impactful when it comes to influence and results. This is a game changer, and why we will spend some time here.

Let's walk through several areas where focusing on these basics will (basically) change your life.

Be brilliant in the basics.

You may have seen a t-shirt or social media post that said something like this: *In a world where you can be anything, be kind.*

Kindness is the most basic of the basics.

In kindergarten, many of us were taught to share toys, not to hit others, to say please and thank you, and so forth. Somewhere since then, adults have lost their way.

In 2018, my family moved from the suburbs of Chicago, Illinois, to central Florida, about an hour northwest of Orlando. None of us had ever lived outside the Midwest.

Marne and I have so many friends in Illinois and Wisconsin, decades of relationships, our heritage and fond memories. Moving wasn't easy, and establishing new relationships with depth takes time.

It was an adjustment.

Although, less years in the making, our children were experiencing the same thing.

My daughter, Nevaeh, was just 6 years old and entering 1st grade when we made our move. She is friendly, outgoing, athletic and smart, so we knew she would make friends. How she did it was so basic, it's noteworthy.

Our family was sitting in our lanai (fancy word used down here for our screened in porch) and our daughter and son were playing in the yard. They were jumping on our trampoline and playing as kids do.

Marne and I were enjoying conversation with one another, watching the kids and experiencing the warmth and sunshine of Florida in our first October in the south. To say we were loving the temperatures compared to what we were used to is an understatement.

As we were relaxing in the moment, we heard our daughter yelling and saw her waving and jumping. She was getting more and more excited, jumping higher and increasing the volume in her screams of joy.

"Hey, hi, come on over...all are invited!"

I said, "Who's invited? What's going on?"

She stops, looks over at us and smiles like she just got up on Christmas morning to her favorite present.

About that time, not one, not two, but three girls appeared. They have come from somewhere beyond the front of our house, and have entered our backyard. They approached the trampoline, jumped up, climbed in (we did have a net for safety) and joined in on the fun.

Nevaeh introduced herself, and they do the same, and the fun commenced.

Kids being kids. Playing, jumping, laughing...joy!

All from one thing.

Kindness.

I was reminded at that moment how simple it is to be kind to another person, even a stranger.

My daughter's actions convicted me. She was being more kind to people that she didn't know than I typically am to some that I do know.

Watching the joy she had with those girls that day was heartwarming. And it wasn't just that day.

For over 2 years, until their family moved away, at least one of those three sisters was ringing our doorbell on a daily basis. The trampoline was the apex center of the fun, although they enjoyed many other activities too.

The adjustment to moving and having to make new friends wasn't left up to someone else. There wasn't a pity party going on nor an expectation that she was owed something.

Nevaeh was kind to others; and her kindness improved her life too.

What a great basic way to a life of excellence.

Here's another example from the business world.

In my travels and all the events I attend every year, I am touched and moved by the people I meet. Their stories are powerful, and are great testimonies of living and working with excellence.

This past year, I connected with a client that has now become like family. They have a really cool culture, and the business is led by twin sisters.

Julianna Morgan is one of the sisters, and leaders, of Atlas Bail Bonds. They are in business to help people when they are in tight spots. Sometimes it's a simple mistake, like they overlooked paying their license plate renewal. Sometimes it's much bigger, a gap in good decision making leads to some trouble.

Either way, their team is there to help.

They want to grow, to serve, to be known for their smiles, customer service and ease of doing business. What a great way to grow any business, right?!

She shared how thankful she and her sister, Ethel Rangel, are for their team members. They both know that the entire existence and success, or lack thereof, is dependent on their associates, who they really believe are part of their family.

Julianna and Ethel have invested in helping their employees be their very best. But maybe not in the way you would expect.

Sure, professional development, technical training and business skills are part of what they do to improve their team. Most organizations do those things.

What impressed me is what they do for the people on a personal level. They choose to be kind to them.

They see them as people who have value. They place great importance on them being as healthy as possible. Specifically, they encourage their team members to be healthy both physically and financially.

And this is on a very personal level.

Dave Ramsey has a program titled Financial Peace University. It helps people get out of debt, set budgets, live within their means, save money and plan for the future. It's amazing, you should check it out if you need help in those areas.

Julianna offers the program to her staff, for free. They encourage them to go through the course and upon successful completion, they offer them a $500 bonus.

As they say on TV, but wait, there's more!

They also do this with a nutrition program. The company pays for the nutrition course. The employees receive the benefit of their improved health at no charge and again, once the course is completed, a $500 bonus is provided.

What a great way to be kind.

What a great way to go above and beyond as a leader.

What a great use of the basics to expand influence and impact results.

This is excellence in action, my friend.

What are you doing today to be kind? How about inviting others to the fun? Maybe it means listening to someone who is struggling.

Or to quote *Avatar*, letting someone know "I see you."

It's so basic. See someone for who they are, say hello, notice their value, invite, listen, and help them be better.

Kindness. The first and most important of the basics.

Next up is something so important that our universities have courses and full blown degrees on the matter.

It's the main impact method for excellence in customer service.

It's something you do literally thousands of times a day via texts, posts, verbal, email, non verbal and more.

Every relationship you desire to be fruitful, every interaction you hope to be positive, every team desiring to accomplish great results rests on the effectiveness of this basic element.

Communication.

Effective, efficient, clear communication.

Near the end of my debacle known as the real estate investment I previously discussed, several situations occurred that demonstrated the importance of communication.

The final property that I was selling had to go through some court proceedings and ultimately a Sheriff sale. On May 1, 2023 the property was sold.

On July 20, 2023, the county recorded the deed transaction and I was legally freed of the property. What a day of celebration that was!

Marne and I were so excited to end the 18 years of pain and financial loss I had caused our family. We were ready to party!

But wait, there's more...

The county office had all of the court instructions for the final payouts. First, they paid the Sheriff for the transaction, then the county property taxes. Up next would be my mortgage lender and the remaining balance to me.

Seems straightforward, right?

Wrong.

After a couple of weeks I noticed the mortgage had not been paid off, so I called the county office. The woman that I spoke to informed me that even though she had all of the instructions from the judge, she needed him to sign the exact dollar amount of the mortgage payout.

This would have been nice to know earlier.

Back to the court we went, and a few weeks later the judge processed the order.

I waited an additional two weeks, still no payoff.

So, I made another call to the office. The same woman, Vicki, answers. She shared that she didn't have the order. Perplexed, I asked her to double check.

She then noticed it was there and the file had been with her for two weeks. She said she would process the checks that day.

A bit frustrating, yet wonderful news. We will finally get this done!

Another two weeks go by and still no payout to the bank.

Now, you can imagine that I'm starting to get a little more irritated.

Another call to Vicki.

"Hi Randy, yes, I did process these two weeks ago, the checks are at my office awaiting pick up."

I tried to remain polite and calm with my response, "The order clearly denotes the address in which to send the checks to, help me understand why they weren't sent?"

Vicki matter of factly states, "Oh, we don't send them unless someone signs a release for us to do so."

"I'm happy to sign those right away," I replied. To which she said she would email me the form.

Three days later...still no form.

"Hi Vicki, it's Randy Fox calling again," I greeted her with a tone slightly annoyed. "I never received those forms."

Vicki quickly says, "Oh, sorry, I'll send them now, what's your email again?"

My mortgage was finally paid off in late October, three full months after I no longer owned the property.

I shortened this story the best I could to give you the idea of the turmoil I went through.

You've been through this. You've had a customer service experience that fell way short.

The learning on our call to excellence is that we have to see what is completely controllable and avoidable, so that we don't do this to others.

From my real estate situation, the county office knew the recording of the sale was completed on July 20th. They could have had a simple process in place to read the order and execute it as noted. If there were questions, they could then ask them to the appropriate parties.

If they need a release signed to mail the check, they state as much with upfront communication.

Each of those calls and interactions with Vicki lacked communication. She had additional information that I didn't know, and she didn't share (or seem to care).

She was rushing me off the phone, just trying to check the box on the next task she needed to accomplish. There were so many opportunities for her to clearly explain the process and help guide me to the resolution with excellence.

Instead, she demonstrated a lack of concern. She appeared to have zero interest in how the timing and outcome affected me, and ultimately showed what we shouldn't do when it comes to customer service.

If we're truthful, we can get this way too.

We are in such a hurry that we just want the task done, the call over, the email sent. As we said before, we have to slow down.

People depend on you, and they depend on and trust your insight, knowledge and experience.

You are what the world is waiting for because when you are serving someone else, they are dependent on you.

I needed Vicki's help. I couldn't resolve this on my own. I had no experience with this type of situation, but she did.

Please give people what they need to be successful. If you don't have the answer they need, tell them you'll get back to them by a specific date and time.

And then get back to them.

Nothing is more infuriating than expecting a returned call, text or email and getting ghosted.

Excellence takes great communication.

That's exactly what one of my new service providers is excellent at doing, great communication. Jessica services equipment and our pool each week at our home. Our service day is Wednesday.

After her team visits our home, they leave a card with everything they did; and other information we need to know.

In addition to that, I've received phone calls and text messages updating me if anything is critical. During Thanksgiving week, I received a text message from her early in the week letting me know our service day would be Tuesday due to the holiday.

This type of communication: clear, prompt, in advance, full of detail gives me comfort that they are competent, that they care, and that they respect and appreciate us as humans.

Sure, they appreciate my business, but you can do your job and get tasks completed and not do so with excellence. You can be rude, lack communication and literally treat the situation and people involved like they aren't very important.

That is how Vicki made me feel. The fact that I had to pay a mortgage for 3 months on a home I no longer owned was an absolutely terrible experience, lacking in excellence and respect on her behalf.

Be like Jessica.

There is no such thing as over communication. Make sure people have the information they need, send it in multiple ways and repeat it as necessary.

Be clear.

Be complete.

Be a clear and complete communicator.

I've been married twice, and over the 30 years of combined

partnership experience, I can unequivocally say, "Communication is the key to every relationship."

We have reached the last of our basic concepts for you to be brilliant in.

In 30 years of officiating, and 9 of those as a coordinator of officials, there are two key elements that separate the good from the elite.

There are two specific basic actions that elevated people quickly to the top.

Communication is the key to every relationship.

Not just to a good level, but the absolute highest levels. People who did this, received the most games, the biggest games, post season conference tournament games, NCAA playoff games, and were trusted as crew chiefs.

I was honored to be one of these types of leaders, yet what was a greater honor was watching and promoting people when they executed these two areas with excellence.

The first one we just addressed. Communication.

Excellent communicators have superb skills with the ability

to listen, to understand and to respond professionally. They possess the art of doing so quickly and calmly, even when there is disagreement.

The second area that separates the good from the elite, those that are excellent in all things, is something that, done poorly, would drive coaches crazy.

It's something that our TV personalities on games will talk about when the replays are shown, over and over again.

They aren't wrong when they comment about desiring similar plays to receive similar calls.

It's very difficult as a player or coach to understand what is allowed or what to do when you don't know what is actually going to be called.

This comes down to one word we hear all the time.

Consistency.

Let's state it again.

Consistency.

Doing the right thing, at the right time, as many times as required.

That's consistency.

If a call is made on a play, a similar play later in the game needs to have the same call made. If not, it's inconsistent.

In your professional life, you are more than likely counted on for consistency in your work hours and days. More so, there are expectations of consistency in your performance and level of competency in getting things done.

Doing tasks well, and doing them on time, everytime, requires consistency.

This goes beyond routines, although helpful. This is about so much more, namely:

- Dependability
- Timeliness
- Responsiveness
- Performance levels remaining high
- Having a plan and sticking to it
- Repeatability in outcomes
- Expectations being met and even exceeded
- And much more!

Here's a simple example:

Let's say you would like to have a nicely groomed lawn. If so, you're like me. I don't want it too tall, or too short.

In order to accomplish this, you need to cut the grass *consistently*.

The plan for your lawn care has to include a similar height and frequency of cut.

If you cut your lawn once per week, this will provide a consistent look.

If, however, you decide to cut the lawn 3 times during one week, then wait about 3 weeks to cut it again, it will grow much higher than desired.

In each scenario above, you cut the lawn 4 times that month, yet the results are vastly different.

It's the same in your work, your relationships and your life. Consistency is a critical factor in delivering excellent results.

My brother lives in southern California, while I live in central Florida. The distance, combined with active children, can make it challenging to see each other in person. Without consistent communication and connecting with one another intentionally, we will lose the quality of our relationship.

We call or text each other often. It keeps us close, informed and part of each others' lives.

If someone is important to you, you need to be intentional about consistently connecting with them.

If your work is important to you (which I'm guessing it is), you need to build daily strategies, workflows and routines that keep you consistently at your best. Here are some questions to ponder:

When is your best time of day to accomplish the most important tasks?

When is your worst time to be in a meeting?

How well do you fuel your mind and body to perform at your highest and best levels?

Do you know what distracts you?

What are you doing to alleviate those distractions?

My daughter plays both travel basketball and volleyball. This is a big commitment for her and us. The teams have hours of practice every week where they work on drills for skill development, as well as, practice their plays.

Over and over again they practice.

The key is that repetition creates a higher level of execution and, you guessed it, consistency.

When players on a team have practiced what to do, and the proper way to do it, the consistency is shown in the outcome.

When they don't execute as planned, it's back to the basics. They have to go back to drills, back to working on what was wrong, so the next time they get it right.

Consistency doesn't just happen, my friend.

Consistency is an intentional act of ensuring your work, your performance, your relationships, and your life aren't on a constant roller coaster.

Consistency requires putting in the time, planning properly, and becoming more consistent in all areas of your life.

Well, there you have it, the most basic elements to be even more brilliant than you could ever imagine.

Three basic elements:

- Kindness
- Communication
- Consistency

When you live a life of kindness, focus on effective communication, and practice consistency, you, my friend, have the basics.

These basic principles aren't easy, yet they are paramount to establishing excellence. They are the foundation on which you can achieve unwavering growth.

Be basic.

Be brilliant.

Be brilliant in the basics.

CHAPTER SIX

The Call to Community

Blue state versus red state.

Vax versus no vax.

PGA Tour versus LIV Golf.

Fox News versus CNN.

Green Bay Packers versus Chicago Bears.

Some things in life are just simple decisions, while others are actually divisive. Unfortunately, too many times our media and culture is fueling divisiveness.

It isn't just a healthy debate. No, it's drama and angered

commentary to get people outraged due to the lack of agreement.

The mantra has wrongly been, "You don't like what I like, so I don't like you."

This needs to stop, immediately!

We need to be creating community, every moment, every day and in every way.

The call to excellence means nothing without a community working together, loving one another, and realizing that no one is better than another.

We can differ, yet still have community.

We can be different, and still have love.

We can see things with a different lens than someone else, yet that doesn't mean we can't find common ground.

It's time to get back to the basics of human respect and decency.

This isn't about conforming to what just one person wants. It's about building a community that works together for the benefit of all. Each doing their part to help make it a better team, a better organization, a better family, a better community and a much better world.

You can take care of yourself and still care enough about others to build a healthy community. There is room for both self-care and selflessness.

In a real community though, there is no room for selfishness.

How do we pursue this excellence in the community?

So glad you asked!

First, we need to change!

> *There is room for both self-care and selflessness.*

In my book *Silver Platter Service*, we highlighted a study that the FoxPoint team conducted in 2020 regarding change. We discovered that the majority of people are either hesitant or resistant to change.

I have continued to ask the question at my speaking engagements. Literally thousands of people continue to confirm that the clear majority of people are *hesitant* to change.

When we ask them about the hesitancy, here are the top responses:

- Don't like new things
- Don't like being uncomfortable
- Fear of unknown
- Don't understand the need to change

Let's hit them quickly one by one.

Go ahead and pick up your device, e.g., your phone/camera/internet/email/social/texting device. Twenty years ago you couldn't do all of that in the palm of your hand. New things aren't so bad, are they?

What about being uncomfortable? Yeah, it's uncomfortable, but you need to get comfortable being uncomfortable. Seriously, there is no way to build muscle without stretching it, and that can be uncomfortable. The payoff though, is worth it. Same thing in your life. Stretch, grow, build...live!

Into the Unknown is a hit song from the second Frozen movie. The entire theme of the song is a call to action into the unknown. It's a rally cry to head out and explore. I'm glad the explorers hundreds of years ago were willing to do the same in our country. Look at what we have and enjoy today based on their willingness to explore new territory.

If you aren't sure of the reason for heading into the unknown, then ask questions. If you know the why, then share that information with those that are hesitant. The best way to understand the need is to have the discussion. Be gentle, be honest, and be open minded.

> *You need to get comfortable being uncomfortable.*

By being willing to change, we can build community. We can explore new adventures, and potential successes by stretching ourselves into the unknown.

We can see this play out in simple, subtle ways and in much larger and obvious ones too. Let's keep our journey rolling and pursue the amazing joy and benefits of real community.

First, a tale of what not to do.

It was May, 1991.

My Chicago Bulls had been improving each year since drafting the GOAT (Michael Jordan, don't even try to say there is anyone better...lol).

In the playoffs the two previous seasons, the Bulls fought hard, yet lost to the The Detroit Pistons, a.k.a. The Bad Boys. They were not nice men. They played dirty, so their nickname was well coined.

These past defeats made it evident the Bulls would have to design a roster and an offensive and defensive strategy that would get them past this physical, rough and bully-like Piston team.

Well, in May of 1991, that's what happend.

In a best of 7 series, the first team to win 4 games advances in the NBA playoffs. In the series between the two teams, it took the Bulls just 4 games to win.

Yep.

A sweep.

Total domination.

One team full of talent and teamwork, and the other just full of "you know what".

Nearing the conclusion of the final game, it was apparent to everyone that the Bulls would easily win.

Both teams took their starters out of the game. With less than a minute to go in the game, all of the Detroit starters walked from their bench at one end of the court, slowly past the scorers table and then they walked past the Bulls bench.

They simply made their way to the exit, and it wasn't pretty.

These dividers of the community left the court with the game still going. They walked directly past the Bulls' starters with disgust.

The Pistons didn't shake hands. They didn't congratulate the winners. They didn't even look at them.

Not one glance.

This cowardly and selfish act was a grandstand moment to make the point, "Look at us, we don't care about you!"

The situation is still one of the most infamous displays of poor sportsmanship in sports history. It goes down as a mark of supposedly grown men acting as spoiled young boys.

The poor modeling of their selfish actions on display to the world was this:

- You can pout when you lose
- You don't owe people anything
- Other people aren't human, they are just in your way
- It's ok to hate someone else

And we wonder why we struggle with community.

This is just one of many examples of absolutely what not to do. Unless, of course, you want to destroy relationships and erode community.

Think about the news you watch, the people you follow, or the organizations you are connected with. Are they creating community by honoring others or are they simply wanting to boast of self?

Do they promote community or promote division?

Do they foster love and kindness or hate?

Even on a personal level, the things we say, the actions we take, and the way we lead, either promotes self or promotes community.

At the time of this writing I traveled to San Diego for a speaking event. For my ground transportation in California, I hired Uber drivers. Two of the drivers left a very contrasting impression on me regarding community.

Upon entering the back seat of my Uber, it is common for me to ask a driver how their day is, and then follow up with a question on how their business is going.

The first driver answered me by sharing stories on how people weren't tipping enough. He complained about how the well dressed business men wouldn't tip much, or at all.

He was also frustrated with his share from Uber, and on and on went his complaints.

As my ride concluded, he got out of the car, retrieved my bags from the trunk and shook my hand. He said that any extra love was always welcome. He then asked me to pull out my phone and check the app. He wanted me to make sure the ride was completed on the app and that I saw the opportunity to rate him and leave a tip.

Now, driver number two.

When I asked him my standard questions, he immediately opened up about his family. He shared his journey from the Phillipines to the United States and how grateful he was to have work. He then asked about my family and the conversations flowed easily.

There was a sign hanging from the back of the passenger seat that said, "Let me know what I can do for you." The images included music, phones, temperature and drinks.

I asked him for a charger, and he handed me a cord with 3 charging options ensuring my device could be properly charged.

As the ride concluded, same drill as driver number one; he got out, retrieved the bags, shook my hand. Yet, this handshake was totally different than that of driver number one.

This gentleman bowed, he thanked me for riding with him and expressed his appreciation of our conversation.

"May God bless you," were his final words to me.

In the Uber app I left both drivers a tip, yet not of equal value or percentage.

Can you guess which one I left a higher tip for?

Interestingly enough, the second driver was the only one of the two that responded to me in the app with a "thank you" for the tip.

I guess I was just another one of the frustrating businessmen to the first driver.

We can see from these examples how simple things make a big impact on others. We must understand that living for ourselves separates us from others.

And that is NOT community.

How you think, the attitude you choose, the words you say, the actions you make and the influence you have is either building up community or building up yourself.

My friend, we need one another. We need community.

We need to offer respect and honor without expectation of reciprocation.

I'm not saying we shouldn't be generous. I'm also not saying you can't be frustrated with a loss.

What I'm saying is that your messaging, your interactions with others, and your ability to change how you approach community matters.

That's what community is about.

You *and* me.

Me *and* you.

All of us together.

In 2009, Marne, our two sons and I voyaged on an amazing Caribbean cruise.

From the entertainment, to the abundant food, to the beautiful scenery, to the wonderful people, to the excursions in Honduras and Bahamas; this was an adventure to remember!

And it was, in so many unexpected ways.

We met another group on the cruise, and became vacation friends (you know the kind, you have a blast together on the vacation, but probably don't stay in touch after).

Marne and I asked them if they would like to go for dinner and dancing one evening.

They were excited, so much so, they invited us to join them the night of their anniversary dinner. A special and unexpected gesture on their part.

They welcomed us into their community.

Before our big adult date night, Marne and I took the boys to dinner. Trevor, our oldest was 11 ½, Brendon was 8.

With some food in their bellies, a show on tv, their favorite games and stuffed animals, they were ready to settle down for the night. We believed Trevor could handle it from there.

Off we went for an elegant dinner with our new friends, it was fabulous. Great food, laughter and a toast to marriage.

Before we headed to the dancing, I politely excused myself from our group to stop by our stateroom. It was about 10 pm, time for lights out for the boys, so a quick check in was the proper thing to do. Remember, it's 2009, so not the same type of onboard communications available today.

The boys were all snuggled in their beds dreaming of sugar plums dancing…not quite.

They were in bed, ready to go to sleep, my timing was perfect to tuck them in and say goodnight. I asked them if they needed anything else, instructed them not to leave the room, to go to sleep and we would be back in a while.

A couple hours later, Marne and I return to our room where we find the lights out, boys asleep…and a full tray of grilled cheese, fries and drinks sitting on our bed. The food had hardly been touched, so we weren't sure what had transpired.

The next morning, we asked the boys where the food came from.

Trevor shared that just after I left the room the night before, Brendon kept saying he was hungry. Trevor reminded him they couldn't leave the room. Brendon was hungry, period.

Turns out that hours earlier, Trevor ate dinner, but Brendon only had ice cream. Marne encouraged him to eat more, but he insisted he wasn't hungry at that time.

Trevor continued to share that he knew they couldn't leave the room, but he wanted to help his brother. He called me on my cell phone, but I didn't answer.

He kept trying, 15 times he called me from the room to my phone. Desperate to find a solution, he then called the customer service desk on the ship.

"Hi, this is Trevor, my parents are out right now, my dad isn't answering his phone, we can't leave the room and my brother is hungry."

The agent on the phone says, "Let me see if I can track your parents down."

The agent looks to see where we have used our card on the ship. They called several locations we had been to, but unfortunately, they just missed us.

After a few minutes, the agent is back with Trevor, "I can't track them down, but I'll send some food to your room. Grilled cheese, fries and some drinks will be up there shortly."

The food arrived about 30 minutes later, but Brendon had fallen asleep. I'm just saying, you can't make this stuff up!

I thanked Trevor for listening to us, for respecting the rules and keeping them safe, and for being creative in his problem solving.

That is...until we were ready to check out at the end of the cruise.

I was the recipient of an unexpected gift...a $75 phone bill. Every one of those calls he made cost $5.00 each!

Note to self: food is free on cruises; however, calls from your room to a cell phone are not.

Once I calmed down from the shock of the bill, we departed the ship and headed back to the realities of life. I turned on my cell phone and checked my messages.

I had 15 missed calls and 15 voicemail messages from Trevor. Each with a bit more anxiety, faster speaking and calls for help.

Marne and I laughed at the entire situation, but felt badly too. We were grateful that in our absence, someone else was there to help.

Community is taking care of one another.

The story reminds me of something we all know, yet need to get back to more often. Community is taking care of one another.

Trevor took care of his brother, the agent took care of them both. We had no idea this was even going on, yet we are grateful for the level of service excellence the representative provided our sons.

No matter the situation we find ourselves dealing with, we can be sure that community is created when we take care of one another.

All of us, living life together.

Not one better than the other, but all unique, valued and special. All caring for each other's needs and concerns.

Try it.

Today.

You can be the person to others that you want others to be to you.

Be bold...go first...answer the call.

Build your community today!

CHAPTER SEVEN

Time for a New Smartphone

In my childhood home, our TV lasted over 20 years.

I've had cars that have lasted over 12 years with nearly 200,000 miles; and I still received money when I sold them!

A bottle of honey will last forever if stored correctly.

We fly in planes that are decades old to see buildings in Europe built hundreds or thousands of years ago.

But, that stinking cellular phone. You're lucky if you get 5 years out of it.

It absolutely amazes me how quickly our cellular devices stop working.

I get it. New apps come along, there are new upgrades in technology, and of course, the manufacturers want to sell new devices. They basically make the old ones obsolete at some point.

I had an "older" phone, like 5 years old, and some apps had stopped working. I went to the network providers' store, and they explained that my operating system was too old to support them.

My options were to give up those specific apps, which I needed, or buy a new phone.

You've been there.

While I'd love to say I have the answers to changing technology, I do know this, some things should LAST.

There are just some things in your life, in your leadership, in your sphere of influence that should LAST.

Roadwork. (I threw this one in there, if you're from the North, you know what I'm talking about.)

Results.

Relationships.

We want these things to LAST.

We desire to have sustained success and meaningful relationships.

LAST

It's an acrostic for the very most important things you can do to position yourself for excellence in your relationships, and ultimately the types of results you achieve.

First is L for Listen to Learn:

In 1996, I was promoted and relocated to a small printing company in West Bend, Wisconsin. The corporation I worked for, Wallace, had just ventured into a new market segment, commercial printing, and Post Printing was our first acquisition.

My role was sales support manager for our national sales team. The role was dedicated to help the new company meld into our culture, and help our Wallace sales team close deals in this new product line.

Within just a few months, we far exceeded our expectations on sales, the growth was very fast. So much so, the president of my new location decided we needed to make some changes; enhancements to our focus on how we conducted our front end operations.

I was promoted again to customer service manager.

My new area of responsibility included managing our estimating, planning, and customer service teams.

These teams had been operating separately, with a previous manager of each area. Estimating handled the initial quote to a client, while planning would put all the details together for the plant once an estimate became a job. The customer service group then worked with the client as the main point of contact throughout the lifecycle of the job.

Three separate teams meant three separate points of contact for the client.

Confusing.

Moreover, it created errors and issues since three different people were speaking to the client, and working on the project in the different phases from conception to completion.

My new role, which was an entirely new one for the company, was to help bridge the gap, create a better workflow, with less errors, and a better overall experience for our clients.

I believed I had the answer.

One contact for all phases.

Each team member would now handle a client from the beginning to the end of a job. They would meet the client's needs by realizing the best way to produce the job. In the end, we could make money versus the estimate, and we could do a better job of exceeding expectations with the client through the production.

Brilliant! Totally brilliant.

I wasn't sure why this hadn't been done before. Why did they always have all of these people with different handoff points?

This new process would give the team members ownership and autonomy, create a better client experience, and reduce errors from poor communication among departments.

No more departments at all. We had a single contact serving their individual clients.

Again, brilliant.

Until it wasn't.

One day, one of my team members, Diane Beth, asked me to come to the conference room with her. I loved Diane, not just because she has two first names, but because she had a great smile and infectious personality. She loved taking care of clients.

She escorted me to the room, which was full (standing room only) of my entire team. There was one seat still open, they left that for me, and ironically, it was at the head of the table.

She said, "Randy, we need to talk. This isn't working. We are overwhelmed, some people have too much work, some have none. And many of us don't have the training and experience to handle the technical parts of the new roles. We need you to listen to us and find a better way."

This was a mic drop way before the phrase was coined.

I looked around the room, saw the eyes and expressions of the team, and realized I needed to listen to learn.

Put the right people in the room, ask the right questions and together, you will discover the best solutions.

They spent the next 30 minutes unpacking the frustrations, concerns and issues the new roles had created for them. And, worse yet, our clients were suffering too.

This is exactly what I *didn't* want to happen.

I shared my purpose and expected outcomes, and the why behind my realignment. I conveyed that the way we were doing things wasn't fast enough, and wasn't making communication and workflow smooth for our clients, nor our plant production team.
They listened and learned too.

Then, the magic happened.

If you want results that last, you need to listen to learn.

Put the right people in the room, ask the right questions and together, you will discover the best solutions.

Next up is A for Attitude:

So much has been written and said about being positive and having a good attitude. There are many cliches when it comes to attitude.

One of my favorites is, "The level of your aptitude will be determined by the level of your attitude." Meaning, if you have a positive attitude, you can achieve positive results.

I'm sure you want some of that!

In reality, when we focus and think about only good things; those that are positive, noble, true, right and helpful, we put ourselves in a better position for excellence. Certainly, having a positive attitude can produce a better day, and one with more influence on others that helps achieve impactful results.

We feel better, we act better, and we relate better with others.

Why?

My friend and speaking colleague, Matt Booth, is an expert on attitude and clarifies this very basic, key fundamental area in our lives.

He says, "Our attitudes form our thoughts, and our thoughts will form our actions."

It's that simple.

Yet it's important, powerful and absolutely a game-changer.

When we focus our attitudes (minds) on good things, we filter situations differently. We see the best in others, we find joy in life, and we can navigate tough times with more ease.

We have literally zero chance of sustained success, or of achieving any real results with excellence, when our attitudes stink. I'm sorry, it's the truth.

How's your attitude?

How do you handle unmet expectations?

What will you do to impact relationships and results by improving your approach, starting with your attitude?

No matter what state you find your attitude in today, we can and need to be better, myself included.

Check your attitude. Your attitude impacts your influence and your influence impacts your results!

Back to my meeting with Diane and the team.

If my attitude was one of being closed off, and negative about their concerns, we would have made no progress.

If their attitudes were only complaining with no approachability, we would have heard whining, not winning.

By remaining open, staying positive and respecting one another (all things people with great attitudes do), we found ourselves well on our way to success.

Just like my team was about to do.

Moving on to S for Serve:

In any relationship, the question that should be paramount to you is this: am I doing (saying) this for the benefit of the team (or other people) or am I doing this solely for my benefit?

Sure, we all do things to improve ourselves. You should always want to be your best. Yet, when it comes to relationships and results, we must (absolutely and unequivocally) ensure that our main objective is to serve.

Serve the other person.

Serve your team.

Serve your community.

Serve the client/customer.

Serve your family.

I said this in my book *You're Missing a Great Game*, and it's worth repeating: it's NOT About You!

It just isn't. If you only focus on yourself, you'll be left with just that.

You.

Alone.

You won't enjoy successful relationships, nor winning with teams, nor finding sustained results.

Those who are there for others, value what it takes to serve with excellence. Things such as:

- Open and honest conversation
- Egos left at the door
- Focusing on the clients, their needs and expectations
- Recognizing facts and figures from fiction and fantasy
- Acknowledging when something is better than what they individually may have wanted or hoped for

Back to our team conversation, our discussion centered around how best to address my concerns for improving our customer service, the new objectives we needed to hit, AND how we could do that effectively for our team.

It came from understanding the importance of serving one another, the customer and our stakeholders.

Service was at the core of our conversation. Not comfort. Not personal victory.

Service.

How could we best serve one another and the client?

In the end, we figured it out!

Together, by listening to learn, with a positive attitude, focused on serving others, we spoke the truth and collectively embraced the best solution.

It's NOT about you!

★★★★★

We implemented a new team circle approach, with three teams in our front office. We actually moved everyone's seats into their new team sections. Everyone went back to the roles they had previously performed, yet without departments.

Each team had two estimators, two planners and two customer service representatives. They all worked together on a designated group of clients to support and serve.

Each team met daily in a formal way early in the morning, yet were so close in proximity to each other that communication improved throughout the day.

Errors went down, our timelines for delivery and response did too, and client satisfaction grew. This new approach was a team collaboration that propelled us to be able to serve more clients efficiently and effectively.

So much so, sales for our company went from 4 to 7 million dollars in revenue in just one year!

You know, this doesn't just happen, it takes intentionality and teamwork. It takes the truth being spoken, recognizing the facts, having a heart to serve others, approaching one another with the right attitude, so people are willing to listen to learn.

The last point, though, is the glue that holds everything that will LAST together.

Last, but not least T is for Trust:

We tend to overlook these powerful strategies that are proven in the workplace and not bring them home. They're actually relationship strategies, so we can use them everywhere, with everyone.

Your personal life and those closest to you are the ones that you focus on first, and most.

Put in the time, the work and the effort to build up your personal relationships. They shouldn't be an afterthought.

Your personal relationships should be top of mind.

We spend so much time at work and tend to come home and give our families the leftovers.

I don't really like leftovers.

Reheated, not fresh, doesn't taste nearly as good.

Help make your personal relationships LAST by bringing a fresh, wonderful, energetic and committed you!

Find ways to energize yourself on the ride home with uplifting music. Take a deep breath before you walk in and actually greet your family with joy. Continue to date your spouse, and play with your kids. Reach out to friends and family and be intentional about remaining connected to them.

Your spouse, children, grandchildren, parents, close friends and others you love, deserve every ounce of effort from you to invest in them.

Your relationship with them should LAST.

Listen to them, have a great attitude towards them, serve them, yet most importantly, they need to trust you.

People need to trust you, period.

Always.

Trust that you have their best interest in mind.

Trust that they can depend on you.

Trust that you will do what you say.

Trust that you will remain loyal and faithful to them.

Trust that you won't neglect or abuse them.

Trust that you will prioritize them over things.

Trust that you will be honorable with your money.

Trust that you won't keep secrets.

Trust what they see and what you say is who you really are.

No one likes to hang around someone they don't trust.

You don't either.

Yet, we can easily get cracks in our relationships by not remaining trustworthy in all of the above, and more.

This isn't the time to turn in a new phone. It's time to answer the call to excellence and invest in those around you by being the one everyone can trust.

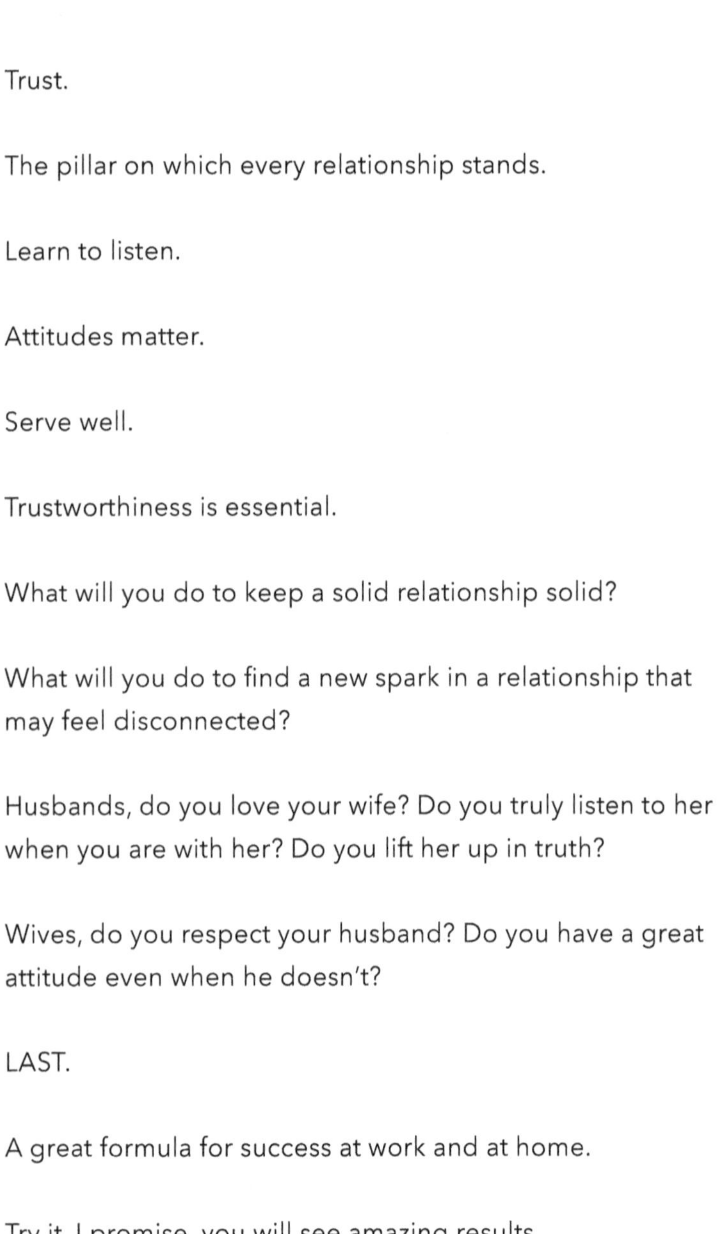

Trust.

The pillar on which every relationship stands.

Learn to listen.

Attitudes matter.

Serve well.

Trustworthiness is essential.

What will you do to keep a solid relationship solid?

What will you do to find a new spark in a relationship that may feel disconnected?

Husbands, do you love your wife? Do you truly listen to her when you are with her? Do you lift her up in truth?

Wives, do you respect your husband? Do you have a great attitude even when he doesn't?

LAST.

A great formula for success at work and at home.

Try it, I promise, you will see amazing results.

CHAPTER EIGHT

Nice haircut!

I risk being vain with this statement, yet here it goes:

I love a great haircut!

When Marne comes home from the salon with a fresh new cut, color or style, it just pops. My eyes are drawn to her and the recently done up locks.

We should want to look good. There isn't anything wrong with looking your best, actually, I'd say that is a pursuit of excellence. When we clean up for others, it shows honor to them.

When we get our hair in place and put on our Sunday best, it shows you have pride in yourself.

A great haircut is a great thing.

A bad one, not so much.

I speak for a living, and being in front of thousands of people every year, I want to make a good impression and look my best.

My hair has always been stubborn, full of collacks and truly has its own personality. And as such, I have always required a really talented stylist to work on the mop.

Why?

Well, so it doesn't look like a mop.

Ivonne was my stylist for nearly 20 years in the greater Chicago area. She was a fabulous stylist. She loved her work and she was a joy to be around.

As the Fox family made our move to Florida, my time with Ivonne came to an end. I still miss having a glass of wine (or two) with her as she did her magic.

Moving across the country has many unexpected variables and stress, yet none compared to the trauma of my hair. I was now in need of a new stylist!

It took me nine months, several tries, many sub par

haircuts, and then it finally happened.

Annie!

I love what she does to make my hair look great. She helps make me look even better than I deserve.

Beyond that, though, what is really impressive about Annie is her approach to service and pure joy for helping others.

As the manager at Symmetry Hair Designs in Belleview, Florida, Annie is responsible for setting the tone for the level of service for the entire operation.

Every six months or so she adds a new apprentice to the team. This new stylist in training shadows Annie, learns the skills to improve as an artist, as well as, the inner workings of their daily services.

As the boss, Annie can direct anyone to do anything at any time. Yet, her approach is so refreshing. There is an obvious intentionality in how she approaches her team, her clients and notably, her words.

One day a seasoned veteran of life walked in the door. She was a slow moving, sweet smiling southern lady. She is a regular in the shop, yet hadn't been in for some time for reasons I didn't need to know.

Annie was working on my cut, and when the woman entered the shop, Annie caught the movement out of the corner of her eye.

"Well hello, my friend, it's so great to see you." Annie continues on with exuberance, " I've missed you! How are you today?"

This is Annie. Not just for that particular moment, every moment.

I frequent the shop often, like every two weeks. I know, I'm a little obsessed with my style, right?

In the nearly 5 years of going there, I've had first hand experience to witness Annie interact with literally hundreds of clients.

Delivering great service once can be easy.

Doing it on an ongoing basis and executing with excellence, well, that's world class.

That's excellence lived out.

Annie has three key attributes that every leader and every human needs in order to be consistent in delivering excellence:

1. *Willingness to teach others*

   How can a team grow, learn and improve without a great leader helping them along their journey?

   It can't.

   You need to be helping others get better. Someone needs to know what you know, and chances are, you need to learn from someone else too.

   Get on it, work to teach, invest and teach others. Someone has done it for you, now it's your turn to do it for another.

> *Delivering great service once can be easy. Doing it on an ongoing basis and executing with excellence, well, that's world class.*

2. *Words of affirmation*

   Maybe you've heard of the Five Love Languages by Gary Chapman. If not, trust me, "words of affirmation" is one of the love languages.

   Not everyone needs this, yet most do. I am one of them.

Even if you are confident in who you are, you want to know what you do matters. You want to know that you make a difference.

Your words matter, and your words to lift up others matter more.

Choose uplifting words that encourage, teach, affirm and build up one another. (More on this later.)

3. *Highest quality service*

    This isn't checking a box, or getting the job done.

    This isn't just meeting expectations.

    This is about exceptional, nothing better, world class service.

    That means it's more than the work being completed, it's how it's completed. People remember experiences, how they were made to feel more than anything else.

    Remember, for something to LAST, service excellence is paramount.

In order to help you with all three of the above, here are just a few common statements, questions and affirmations I have heard Annie express:

To team members:

- When you have a minute, can you help me with something?
- If you look closely, check out what we are working on here with this cut. Do you see what we are doing to make sure this looks great?
- Thank you so much for doing that, you are the best, appreciate you!

To clients:

- You are one of my favorites, thanks for coming in today!
- You simply have made my day, so great to see you.
- That blouse looks wonderful on you, what a great color for your hair and eyes.
- I'll come in on my day off to squeeze you in so you look fabulous for your next event! (that was to me, my schedule moves around rapidly and she always makes it work)

Let's be clear here, this is more than just words.

Annie smiles, she hugs, she asks questions, she listens, she sings. Seriously, she has music playing and sings while she works.

Maybe Snow White and the Seven Dwarfs knew something after all!

Beyond just her actions, there are other examples of the excellence Annie and her team demonstrate.

The shop is always clean, smells great, and everyone is dressed nicely. They don't all wear the same thing. They have their own personality, yet they look comfortably professional.

Let's go back to the music in the shop for a brief moment. In any setting, music sets the mood, it changes everything.

I am literally sitting here listening to worship music while I write this. The music in the shop is the same.

Uplifting music uplifts. Maybe you just need a little good music.

You might be thinking, well, this is her business, so she does these things for people because they pay her.

True, it is her business; yet trust me, this is her at the core of her being.

I believe I know where it comes from too.

Annies' father, Bob, is our parking lot greeter at church. He stands outside every Sunday for 45 minutes, waving his hand as people drive in (which is covered with a big white Mickey Mouse type hand). He then greets them with a smile, and kind words, "Great to see you this beautiful morning and glad you are here!"

Reminder, I live in Florida. It's 85 plus degrees and 70% humidity for like 7 months.

Yet, there is Bob. Faithful to serve and glad he gets to do it. As he says to me, "I'm waiving for Jesus!"

There's something about serving with excellence and realizing you are doing it for something, and someone, greater than you.

I'm not sure what you can do differently than how you currently do it, yet these are simple things that you can do, today.

I encourage you, my friend, to really think and strategize on what you can do to improve your words, your actions and your service to others.

Maybe you haven't thought about this, but you're literally obligated to do so.

You need to work with excellence, always.

No matter your profession, no matter where you live, no matter your age; you can make a huge difference in your team, and for those you serve, simply by raising your level of excellence.

A great way to think about how you can deliver excellence is by asking yourself:

- How do you want to be greeted?
- How do you want to be treated?
- What do you need from others when you feel down, and can barely make it through a day?
- How does it make you feel when someone expresses real care, concern and love for you?

Hopefully, this should be easy for you to implement.

CHAPTER NINE

Love 'em, love 'em and hug 'em

For nearly 20 years, Larry Dietz has been the General Manager of Professional Plating (PPI) in Brillion, Wisconsin.

His great team is mentioned in my book, *Silver Platter Service*, and we just have to share some more.

I actually wrote this as I sat in one of their offices on a beautiful August day. It was their annual company fun day; a tradition to celebrate success and to inspire the winning team. The day is on the calendar for months and is a highly enjoyed and anticipated experience for the entire PPI team.

The day includes:

- A big outdoor tent
- Music blaring

- Fresh food from a local BBQ truck
- Cold Stone treats
- A new company t-shirt for every employee
- A gift card of $25 (or more) for every employee
- Cornhole tournament for some camaraderie and friendly competition
- And oh yeah, little old me

For 10 years I've been honored to share a message on leadership and service excellence at PPI. It's a real pleasure to be invited back so many times. I truly feel like part of their culture and family. Side note, it encourages me to always create new material too.

As Larry and I were catching up that day, he said something that resonated with me.

"Business and great teams are all about culture, Randy." Larry continued, "it's about how we love 'em, love' em and hug 'em."

Love 'em, love' em and hug 'em, it's such a great phrase.

The list of things they do every year at this annual picnic isn't that expensive, yet very impactful. It sends the message that they love their people.

What are you doing with your team to be creative, intentional and purposeful in showing them love?

Here are a few suggestions if you're struggling with ideas:

- Find someone to praise publicly - it can provide much needed fuel at no cost to you
- Smile at people as you walk by - look them in the eye when you do it
- High five people with joy and energy
- Be generous with people, if you're able to - pay them well, give unexpected bonuses and pay for lunch from time to time

In 1997, my first son was born on Saturday, November 1st. Our little bundle came 3 weeks early, so we weren't expecting the life change at that moment.

I called my company President later that day at his home and shared the news. He was absolutely elated for us. He told me to enjoy the week with my son and wife and to cherish the moments and memories.

I thanked him and did just that.

When I came back to work a week later I asked him if he had recorded the vacation time. He replied with love, "Nope, we aren't going to. We are happy for you and wanted you to have that week with your family."

Amazing.

Unexpected.

A great gesture of love.

Fast forward to January of 2012, my youngest, and only daughter was born. I texted my direct manager, the company Vice President, and shared our exciting news.

He was thrilled! He also has one daughter and had previously shared how special the father-daughter relationship would be for me.

Again, I took the week off to be with my family.

A few weeks later, I went into our online vacation system to plug in another set of dates off for a family vacation.

To my surprise, I had 5 days less vacation time than I thought.

No one said anything to me about it, I just found it in the system.

After a little digging, I discovered the human resource director had gone into my account and subtracted the 5 days.

To say I was a bit miffed is an understatement.

From these two experiences, which one do you believe provides a better outcome for the employee relationship?

I understand wanting to have consistent policies, yet policies also remove humanity if not done properly.

Not communicating to me, well, that's certainly not what I would consider doing things properly. Someone needed to speak to me, or at least notify me, about the vacation days being removed.

Not a good relationship builder.

In my travels and working with teams around the country, I'm finding a new trend over recent years.

More and more professionals don't have any vacation time.

That's right.

Zero.

Oh, it's not what you think.

They do take time off, it just isn't tracked.

They are trusted to get their work done. They take time off

for personal and family reasons as needed.

The work, the results, and the impact are what matter.

Not all positions can do this, I understand, but if you can, think about it.

What can you do?

What policy is getting in the way of building a culture of trust?

Loving people requires that we trust them.

You hired them because they are talented. Start trusting them.

In a world with more and more people working remotely, you need to build trust. Tracking their every move, or every hour they work isn't trust.

I really think it's time we think about how we handle things like this in our professional lives.

We also need to consider how this applies personally, too.

Carve out time for those you love.

Treat them with love.

People don't just know you love them because you *say* you love them, they know you love them because of *how* you love them.

Not many folks on their deathbed wish they had worked more. Not many folks will look at their adult children and say they were glad they worked on Saturdays and played golf with buddies on Sundays, and missed out on their kids being kids.

Trust me, I know, because that WAS me! That was Old Randy (you'll get to know him more in the next chapter.).

Until life (well God) really woke me up.

> *People don't just know you love them because you* say *you love them, they know you love them because of* how *you love them.*

Nearly 20 years ago, the following transpired in a 5-year span of my life:

- Very tragically, I lost my first wife to cancer at age 36
- God came into my life and showed me real love
- I married another great woman and she adopted my young sons

- We moved, found friends and fellowship in an amazing new neighborhood and church

- We had a daughter I never expected to have

Life changing.

The process of loving God and loving people changed me. It brought excellence into my life personally and professionally.

I still play golf, yet not on Sundays. There are other priorities in my life that are ahead of that.

These are my priorities and the order in which I aim to live them out: Faith, family, friends, FoxPoint and fun.

What are your life priorities?

Who do you want to spend the most time with?

Do you spend time with them?

What choices are you making to love well, at work and at home?

Your work and your story may be different, yet I hope you don't wait to live out these truths.

Hug often.

Live with a smile on your face and a song in your heart.

Love others well.

This is a call you need to accept, make and live out.

> *Invest in those you love, often, and truly reap the blessings of life!*

Loving others.

This is the path to excellence.

The world, unfortunately, doesn't take this path.

Our world is full of divide, hate and evil. People are selfish and greedy. The reason?

Just love of self. Not love for others.

But, with love, everything changes.

With love, we treat people as:

- Valued
- Heard
- Important
- Respected

In love, we show and give people:

- Forgiveness
- Kindness
- Grace
- Empowerment

And then, people who are loved have:

- Joy
- Belonging
- Purpose
- Love for others

Love.

A beautiful thing.

The world needs more of it.

And the world is waiting for you to bring it.

Time is precious, my friend, there are no do overs.

Invest in those you love, often, and truly reap the blessings of life!

Go love 'em, love 'em and hug 'em!

CHAPTER TEN

Every ~~Book~~ Life Needs Margin

It's impossible and not practical to print a book without margins.

I have a degree in technology (printing proficiency) and spent 20 years in the industry. With that knowledge and experience, I can attest to the above statement.

A printing company cannot print and cut precisely enough, with repeated consistency, to ensure all words are still on the page unless there are margins.

Without margin, how would you read what is bound at the spine? The letters would be cut off.

And finally, margin makes it easier for you to read (and for me to write, plus it adds to the page count).

Margin is a good and necessary thing when it comes to printing and reading books.

Margin.

You may not have thought about it as you read this, yet check it out. Margins in this book are good.

Why is it then that when it comes to our lives, margin is as foreign as an astronaut under the sea?

I've been the drum major for this band of no margin.

I have always wanted to do everything.

Full schedule, great.

Run from one thing to another, super!

Maybe run a bit late to appointments, it's all good, they know I'm busy and important.

And the list goes on.

From early on in life, and far into my adulthood, I ran my life at a furious pace.

No room for more? Ha! There's always room for more.

I believed that being busy was best.

I had no idea what it meant to say "no".

My mom would always say, "Randy, you can't do it all." And when she would say that, my response would be the same, "Oh, just watch me!"

Now, let me be very clear here, I did great work.
I accomplished a lot, provided for my family, and truly enjoyed many aspects of my life.

The reality though, was that I slipped up. More than once.

Things happened that weren't excellent and I (and maybe others) suffered as a result. I know too, that I didn't maximize my performance or life.

Then things changed. Nearly 15 years ago Marne introduced me (Old Randy) to the concept of margin in our lives.

She believed that it was necessary to function at one's best, and more importantly, to have true fulfillment in life.

I wasn't so sure at first. See, I knew that by creating margin in several areas of my life, choices would need to be made.

Tough choices.

Good would be given up for the best.

The dreaded word "no" would have to be said sometimes in order to have the fabulous *"yes."*

In short, though, she was right. Very right.

Life is more full when there is margin, and that allows for the best choices, the best energy levels and the best results. The New Randy knows this from personal experience.

How?

I'm glad you asked.

Since adding margin to my life, I have a higher capacity for performance. Margin allows room to grow, and adapt to life, and has ultimately brought a level of joy in my life that is more complete.

The three areas of margin we will address are:

1. Talent
2. Treasure
3. Time

There are so many good causes to be involved in. There are plenty of good jobs out there. There is always something and someone you can be lending your **talents** to.

Your talent is something special that makes a difference in the world. A wise investment of your talents can change the world.

Regardless of how talented you may be, if you over commit to causes, organizations, people, etc., eventually you will not deliver your best work.

You must choose wisely.

Sometimes saying no to something good leads us to something even greater.

Many years ago, my family attended a church of nearly 750 people located in the far northwest suburbs of Chicago.

Our lead pastor had been on staff with us about 2 years, and he was making great strides in growing, connecting and leading our church.

He came to me one day and asked if I would be willing to voluntarily lead our first impressions ministry. This would include all of the people from the parking lot, to the greeters, cafe, to ushers and more.

He believed my communication skills, ability to lead and energize people would be perfect for the role.

I was honored.

What I didn't know at the time was if I had the capacity or desire to make this level of commitment.

Old Randy would have just said "yes," without too much thought.

Thanks to Marne, New Randy had learned to slow down enough to pause, think, pray and discuss with her.

Even though it was a needed role and I could help, something was telling me it wasn't a good fit. This just didn't seem like something I would love, nor would it be the best use of my skills and talents.

I politely declined the ask.

Typically, when you decline, they move on and you may not be asked again to lead anything. I was okay with that outcome if it happened.

But it didn't.

Several months later, the pastor was back, with a different ask.

This time he had a much more influential role, with strategy, direction and a higher calling involved.

We have talked about accepting calls, and this was one I never dreamed of.

He asked me to join the directional leadership as an Elder of the church.

Wow!

Even with 20 years of corporate leadership in my pocket, I never thought I would be *that* type of leader.

I am just a broken guy that tries, yet fails, but has a heart to serve. I read through the biblical requirements of an Elder in the book of Titus and spoke to my pastor about my findings.

I shared that this standard is not something I can honestly say I do perfectly all the time. I try, but God delivers me over and over again.

His response, "That's exactly why we are asking you! You get it, you know that it is God leading you, and you are working to live out the goals and direction He has in your life."

After 4 years at that church as an Elder, I moved to Florida. That experience gave me the opportunity to then help launch a completely new church in Florida and assist my friend to lead and grow this new congregation.

The preparation positioned me for an opportunity. But it doesn't happen if I hadn't said no to the first ask.

See, the good was good, yet we are after the best.

Excellence isn't found in doing everything, it's found in doing the best thing.

On to our next area in margin, oh, this is gonna be fun.

As they say in the South, I'm about to get up in your living room.

Up close and personal...ready?

Good!

One of the greatest areas of anxiety and strife in life can be finances or **treasure**. Unfortunately, too many divorces happen due to issues related to money. Lives are ruined by financial crisis.

We can all get overwhelmed by the need to work for income, the rising costs of inflation, and never ending pressures to keep up with the Jones', but there's good news.

Actually, it's great news!

Excellence isn't found in doing everything, *it's found in doing* the best *thing.*

There is a solution to the madness.

Margin.

You have treasure, and having a plan that includes margin will bring freedom.

The topic of money is mentioned over 2,000 times in The Bible, more than any other subject. That shows how we handle money is important; it's really, really important.

My grandfather was one of the most influential men in my life. His guidance on money included many one liners, such as:

> "A penny saved is a penny earned."
> "It's not how much you make, it's how much you spend."
> "Don't keep all your eggs in one basket."
> "Don't spend more than you make."

To read more about his wisdom, check out my book *A Leader Worth Following*.

He was talking about margin.

I'm not a financial planner, yet if you need help, contact me and I'll put you in touch with mine. With that as my disclaimer, here are some very practical ways to put margin in your money (treasure):

1. Build (and stick to) a budget. Determine what you make each month, then make a list of everything you need to spend money on, e.g. rent, mortgage, insurance, groceries, entertainment, etc. Some costs will be fixed and others will be based on the income you have left. The real key is not to go over budget, ever. Only spend what you have.

2. The first line item on your budget should be giving money to others. My family gives our first 10% to our church. We also support other ministries and kids all around the world. We believe giving to others is vitally important.

3. The second line item on your budget should be paying yourself first before you pay anyone else, e.g. your savings. You need to save some of your treasure because you never know how life will hit you with an unexpected bill. If you can, save at least 10% (some short-term, some long-term) but the more the better.

4. Live off of the balance. Simply put, live off of what you have left after the above is paid. Did I say don't go over? I thought so...

My friend, most people struggle because they don't live off of what they *have*, they live off of what they *want*. There is no room for error, or something unexpected in their plan, if they even have a plan.

This is why margin is so key in your treasure.

Trust me, early in my adult life, Old Randy was in big time debt, and it stunk.

It's hard work to pay all of those bills.

When you get to a place with no debt, it's amazing.

That outcome may seem like an impossible task, yet the journey starts by creating some margin. Room to give, to save, to pay things off, to fix the car, mend a broken arm, or pay 40% more for insurance, gas or eggs.

Life is an unknown, uncontrollable adventure. The same is true when it comes to your costs.

Build a plan that provides some margin and you will be forever changed. If you are married, do it together.

It truly is a call to excellence.

Finally, the hardest one of all.

Your **time**.

Time is unlike the other two areas, talent and treasure.

Talent you can improve upon and treasure, you can make more of, but time slips away day by day, hour by hour, minute by minute with no help from anyone.

In fact, you don't even know how much of it you have (in years).

How you invest your time is your greatest area of impact in your life.

Time.

How you choose to invest your time.

Notice, this is a choice. Your choice.

Oh, I know you have work to do, and probably five days a week. You may have kids to drive around too, and you need to find time to shop, eat and sleep, among many other things.

> *How you invest your time is your greatest area of impact in your life.*

I am not naive enough to say this is easy.

I am strongly stating, though, that how you choose to spend and invest your time is critical to excellence in your life.

Not only is this true in your life, it's true for any organization.

Again, how *you choose* to invest your time is critical.

Three key points to building margin in your time include:

- you need time to take care of your mental and physical health
- you need time to rest
- you need to focus on the next right thing

The first element is to understand it's impossible to sustain success if you aren't functioning at your best. You need to choose some time for yourself.

A great suggestion, start your day your way.

Don't allow texts, media outlets, social media feeds, emails and such to dictate how you start your day. I recommend staying away from them for at least 15 if not 30 minutes at the start of your day.

You need to begin in a place where you can get ready for the day. Pray, read, meditate, take a walk, sit outside, have a cup of coffee...do what helps you be your best.

Start your day your way.

If you allow those other elements in too soon, your brain, your thoughts and your actions will begin to work on what others want. Your stress will rise and you will be anxious and not as driven in the right direction that day.

Be sure to carve out time for you each day.

Literally set a meeting in your calendar for yourself, that no one else can book. Do it daily.

When I was a VP of Operations, I carved out 4pm to 5pm. No meetings, no access. The door was closed and I went to work on the important elements in order to wrap up my day.

You also need time to work out. When, you may ask?

Whenever!

Years ago I had a personal trainer that said the morning was the best time to work out for the day's energy. However, she noted, the best time to work out was the time you would do it!

Second step in creating margin in your time, you need to take time to **rest**.

You. Need. Rest.

You need naps, sleep, a break from work each day. You also need longer breaks throughout the year.

When was the last time you took a vacation? I mean, getting away, not working and just enjoying people and things you love.

Get to it.

Build margin and energy by getting rest.

The first two points are key to your ability to maximize your time, yet there is one more.

If you struggle with the first two, stop reading until you're ready for more.

Our third step in margin in time is the one that truly utilizes your time the best.

Focusing on the next right thing.

Focus is key to success and is a major step to excellence.

The number one way to be at your very best in any given moment, is to be in that moment!

Stop multitasking.

Old Randy used to think doing five things at once made him smart, talented and efficient.

I was just doing multiple things simultaneously at a lower level than my best.

Not excellent.

New Randy knows better.

If you need to switch tasks, then switch. Fully.

Don't keep doing multiple things at the same time.

I am on so many video calls with people who are also reading emails, looking at their phones, texting, and sometimes even talking to others.

Notoriously, they come back with an apology for missing what was just said. They tell us they are good to go, until someday down the road they question why things are happening. UGH, so frustrating!

Focus means to focus on the task, the opportunity, the work and, most importantly, the people currently in view.

People deserve your attention. They want to know they are heard and respected.

How can you possibly do that if you are literally doing five things at one time?

We aren't that good, sorry, we just aren't.

What a better world we would have if we got off of our devices and looked someone in the eye? If we leaned in and listened.

Spend time focusing on the one thing or person that needs you right now.

You will be amazed how fast, and how much better, you accomplish things.

Believe me, I was there...and now I work hard to not be scattered.

Margin is your friend.

Margin gives you energy, health, a better attitude and the ability to work with efficiency. That combination leads to effectiveness and effectiveness drives results.

Put it all together, margin is key to sustaining your excellence.

My friend, the book of your life needs margin.

Maybe you're doing great in a couple of these areas, yet, if you're honest, I'm sure there is one that you need to work on.

Write it down here in the margin →
(you see what I did there?), and put it in your workbook.

What steps will you take in the next 5 days to improve the margin in either your talent level, treasure investment or time allocation?

Take time to look at this, don't rush.

As you look strategically at how you invest your talent, treasure and time, things will change. Margin will increase and so will your performance; which in turn, will improve the fulfillment in your life.

Now that's something most excellent!

CHAPTER ELEVEN

Irreplaceable

Many times over my career and travels, I hear people complaining about the opportunities they aren't getting, and the issues that keep them and their teams from succeeding.

The whining and frustrations pour out of them with a nasty aftertaste. They simply can't seem to quench the thirst of anger.

And typically, they blame others for their lot in life.

The list is long, yet here is a snapshot of the leadership headaches and complaints I've heard:

- Mean people
- Lack of communication

- Poor direction
- Late people
- No shows
- Rude people
- Unappreciative folks
- Lack of training
- Outdated technology
- Policies that make no sense, at least to them
- Not enough resources
- Unreasonable demands of others

I think you get the idea.

Here's my point...

You can't control most of these things. Oh, you can control what you do in these areas, but you can't control others.

You may not be able to control what they do and say, but you can influence them.

You need to control what you can control.

As we said previously, your thoughts, words, actions have influence and that is how you impact excellence.

Even though the list (which is actually much longer in reality) is vastly beyond our control, we tend to perseverate on these things.

Don't do it!

You're wasting your time and energy focusing on negative things. Stop thinking and complaining about things out of your control.

Stop blaming others.

Now, as it's up to you, if you can change people and processes in your team for the better, do that for sure. But the real place to focus is your own behavior and attitude.

Work on you.

Work to eliminate all the things on the list from your behavior. Be the one who models the desired expectations, and you will be a force of influence that drives better results.

In the early 2000's, as plant manager, I was responsible for a manufacturing facility, the employees, all activities and outcomes.

This meant that everything was under my direction and responsibility. From profit/loss, to product quality, to employee productivity, to on-time delivery results, to safety numbers and more, it was on me to lead us in our progress.

My vice president at the time was known for a phrase that

instilled the ownership and authority of a plant manager. He would say, "Don't be a victim!"

QUICK TIMEOUT: I am not saying that we don't have victim situations in our society. People are abused, mistreated and abandoned. This is NOT the type of victim we are talking about. If you are a victim of someone else physically or emotionally hurting you, please call the professionals. There is help and hope for you. Do not stay in that situation.

TIME IN: Breaking this down, the VP meant what I just said on the previous page: don't complain about things or people you can't control. Don't sit back and blame others about everything going on around you, or what you don't agree with or dislike.

On the contrary, the VP was urging us to step up to excellence. A call to stop believing that you can't change anything or don't have the ability to make a huge difference.

You need to step up to deliver results, be creative, work hard, and work through situations to solve problems. This is a call to accept responsibility for yourself and those you manage.

The call is not to sit down in the mud and say, "I'm in the

mud, poor me, look at me in the mud, someone put me in the mud."

Get up, walk forward, do what you can and need to do, and make yourself irreplaceable.

Yes, I'm talking about making yourself that valuable.

Irreplaceable.

Just getting the job done is checking a box. That isn't excellence.

Showing up is good, but it's not good enough. And just good enough isn't good enough for our call to excellence.

Be irreplaceable!

Be so valuable that no matter what happens, you're still there.

Changes in direction in an organization? You're still there.

Cut backs happen? You're still there.

New leadership comes in? You're still there to step up, get on board with the new plan, and become a key component of the new found success.

New ways of doing things come around? You're still there to adapt, grow, teach and lead the way.

Sounds hard, doesn't it?

It is.

Yet, that's what the pursuit of excellence is...HARD!

If pursuing excellence was easy, everyone would be doing it.

Simple truth, most people are not willing to put in the work required for excellence.

I'm so glad you are here with me to take this journey and accept the call!

Check out this true story:

My niece, Brenna, works in the musical industry in New York. If you aren't familiar with musicals, they are live performances done on stage, typically with a grand story, singing, amazing music, and spectacular wardrobes and set designs.

London has the West End, New York has Broadway, and Chicago is the Second City. Many of these shows travel the world and have entertained people for decades, such as,

Phantom of the Opera, Cats, Les Miserables (my favorite), *Annie, Lion King* and *Aladdin*.

Aladdin is a classic Disney tale of a street rat (a boy) that becomes a prince thanks to the genie in the bottle, and he ends up marrying the princess. Well, their story isn't without its issues, but in the end it all works out.

This is where Brenna now works. In the back of the house, on the wardrobe team for the stars of *Aladdin*. If you go to the theater and see the show, you will never see her.

So many of our jobs and roles in life are like hers. You find yourself doing something important, yet not many know about it, or ever give you the standing ovation. I get it, remember, I was an NCAA basketball official for 23 years. No fans in the stands ever applauded my work.

Brenna has been working hard for many years to make it to Broadway. She has had temporary gigs and times of no gigs at all. She supplemented income as many do, yet her passion and dream is to be excellent at her craft in the wardrobe department.

There are 15 characters in the live production of this show, and 15 full time wardrobe staff to work on them during the show. You know, when the quick costume changes happen, there is someone standing off stage, in the dark, ready to help the stars of the show make their necessary changes.

Being at the correct location off stage with the exact timing, combined with the wardrobe staff's ability to execute the costume changes, is paramount to a successful show. Each character has different tracks of where they will be and which costume is next, and it's up to their wardrobe specialist to make it happen.

Every.
Single.
Time.

For one, if not two shows a day, six days a week.

Brenna was fortunate enough to be added as part time staff for the show. She made spot number 16.

As she began to work, she realized that most of her team would know the track for a couple, maybe a few of the characters. Meaning, they could work on Aladdin, or Jasmine, or the Genie.

Brenna wanted to get on full time. She wanted to be done with the days of not knowing what would be next and how she would pay her bills.

This show has run for years and will run for years to come, so she saw an opportunity to become a more permanent part of it.

She started learning the work involved in the entire show, and was willing to do whatever it took to be excellent, as well.

That meant sewing, cleaning dirty, smelly costumes, whatever. Not fun, yet all in was she (that's my best Yoda).

As Brenna began to fill in for full time staff, she learned more and more about the characters. She quickly realized that no one knew the tracks to all 15 characters. Actually, not even close, no one really knew more than half of the show.

Brenna could have been a victim. She could have complained about the process, the decisions, the lack of full time work. She could have complained about anything and everything.

Instead, she went to work.

Her moment of excellence was that she learned it all. She is the only one who knows all 15 characters.

> *If pursuing excellence was easy, everyone would be doing it.*

Irreplaceable.

For over a decade, this show has had 15 full time employees

in this capacity. Recently, the show's producer asked the director, "Why do we need another full time wardrobe swing at this point?"

The show's director responded with, "We simply can't do it without Brenna."

So, now there are 16 full time staff.

That, my friend, is irreplaceable.

That's answering the call to excellence.

CHAPTER TWELVE

Every Day is a Saturday!

Most people I know love Saturdays.

Our culture has embraced the "working for the weekend" concept, so Saturday receives higher honor than other days.

Even though Sunday is still the weekend, Sunday is too close to the dreaded Monday. People start getting stressed around 3 p.m. thinking of all they have to do that coming week.

Friday is a great day too, but many still go to school and work, so they tend to be tired at day's end.

For the vast majority of people, Saturday is the day of freedom! It's a day off from work, from school, and from all the normal mundane routines.

Saturday is a fun day; a date night, a ball game, a movie, a chance to sleep in, a day to do more of what you want. What a great day!

My purpose in this final chapter is to change your perspective. What if we approached each and every day like a Saturday?

We have to find joy in every day, not just Saturday.

The call to excellence isn't about enjoying one single day and just surviving the other six. The person who lives out excellence finds their Saturday every day.

We will walk through three concepts you can embrace and employ in your life that will help you live each day more abundantly. A life that is more full, with more joy, and with more impact.

You want some of that?

Oh, I know you do...let's bring this baby home!

I have a friend that has enjoyed over 55 years of life. Most of her life has been wonderful, yet, like you and me, there is more to her story.

The person who lives out excellence finds their Saturday every day.

There have been hard days, hard years, relationship concerns, financial worry; you get it, you've been there.

Our stories, in reality, aren't all rainbows and unicorns.

I may not know your story, yet I know you have faced situations where doors have closed. Maybe you have been fired from a job, or had the love of your life break up with you, or had your financial investment backfire, or gotten into an accident when you were already late…you get the idea.

You have a story and maybe your story wasn't always wonderful, or maybe you are currently struggling with some real issues. Either way, this is for you.

It's for us all.

Live in the NOW!

We need to recognize the value in living in the present moment. The past is gone, the future isn't here yet, so we need to live in the now.

Live your best and most excellent life at this very moment. As the great Dr. Suess says, "you never know the value of a moment until it becomes a memory."

By the way, thanks for spending these moments with me.

I'm not quite finished, though.

NOW stands for something. My friend shared this acronym with me, and she gave me permission to share it with you.

It's such a great reminder that when one door closes, a window just may open. Living a full and abundant life isn't wallowing in the mud. We have to change our perspective, be on the lookout for another path and seize the day.

Live in the NOW...the Newly Opened Window.

Stop banging on the door that closed. Stop trying to break it down. Instead, climb through to the next opportunity.

It's time to look around and see all of the wonderful things, the people, and the opportunities in your life. It's time to be brave, and be willing to take a new, exciting step.

This is the only moment that matters; the NOW moment.

Live in the NOW!

★★★★★

Live in it!

Practically speaking, your attitude and perspective are certainly important, but your willingness to refuse to be stuck, trapped and negative is more important.

A positive approach will make everyday just a little better, maybe even more like a Saturday.

Which brings us to our second piece of advice for making everyday a Saturday.

I was told to avoid saying never or always. They are too absolute, setting a standard we can't meet.

Well, I'm going to say them anyway. It's that important. This is the highest call and we need to set great boundaries to get great results.

Two things in life we should never, ever, ever do.

These two things hold us back, build anxiety, destroy our confidence, and make us feel worthless.

Two things that you and I should never, ever, ever do:

Compare and complain.

Say it out loud. Never, ever, ever...

Really, say it out loud.

I will never, ever, ever compare or complain.

"Dad, but she's on her phone, why can't I be on mine?"

A very typical whiny comparison and complaint from a younger sibling about her older sister.

I witnessed this first hand. The dad, who's a great friend of mine, said this is a daily occurrence. One wants what the other has and doesn't understand why they can't have it.

I've been there. You've been there.

Kids are amazing experts in how to compare and complain.

But it does them no good. None at all.

Their tone, the constant comparison and complaining changes absolutely nothing about their circumstances. Actually, it just frustrates them and their parents.

I shared with my friend an idea that he should ask the younger one to do the math homework of the older one. With several grades in between them, she has no chance to do the math beyond her years.

He said to me, "Oh, that's a good one."

And it's good for you, too.

See, the idea that you should get what others have, or that

your life should be like theirs, is preposterous. You have gifts, talents, a family and a life that are uniquely yours. *You* need what *you* need to live *your* best life.

Complaining changes nothing. It just makes you angry.

Comparing changes nothing either. It just makes you depressed.

Remember: never, ever, ever compare or complain.

A practical tip in this regard: don't spend too much time trolling people on social media. Their best life is out there, and very little of the reality and hard stuff gets posted.

When was the last time you saw a post that said, "hey, life is hard, got fired today, my wife left me, I'm in debt up to my eyeballs, the house just got foreclosed, who wants to be me?"

Let's not spend any more time on what we shouldn't do, instead let's move on to what we should be doing. Our final piece to make every day a Saturday.

It's Christmastime as I write these pages, and one of the most famous movies of all time is also a musical by Irving Berlin. I'm referring to the timeless classic *White Christmas*.

Bing Crosby dancing with Danny Kaye, a great tale of

falling in love, navigating challenges, and the power of music bonding people together. In the end, all is great, the costumes are lovely, the general is honored, and our guy and girl fall in love.

There are many popular songs from the movie that we still sing today, including *White Christmas*, which I only dream of now since I live in Florida. There is another catchy song that Bing Crosby and Beverly Clooney (the aunt of George) sing.

The tune *Count Your Blessings (instead of sheep)*, is such a great reminder of what you and I must do.

This is our third and final way to live everyday like a Saturday.

This is a currency exchange of the best value.

You never, ever, ever compare or complain; instead, you must always and forever count your blessings and compliment others.

What a difference it is when we stop complaining about things and people out of our control, and we start counting the blessings we have in our lives.

I know life is stressful, yet when you are worried and can't sleep, count your blessings instead of sheep.

That's a line from the song, and it works.

Many years ago a friend of mine suggested that I write down all of the blessings in my life. Then, each day, read the list of blessings and add more to them.

Eventually I stopped the routine, but only after hundreds of items, people, happenings and more were counted. It was a truly therapeutic process, and one that revealed that I have so much to be thankful for.

Try it for yourself. Write the list, read it daily, and add more to it as the days and weeks go by.

Always and forever be counting your blessings.

The other part of our always and forever mindset and currency exchange, is to compliment others. Kinda hard to do if you're comparing yourself to others.

We need to see the value others bring, and shine a spotlight on them when it's deserved.

Don't you love it when someone compliments you?

It can be about simple things like your hair, your attire, or a meal you made, to more complex things like your personality, your work performance, or how you handled a really tough situation.

Being valued, feeling like you have worth, that you make a difference, and that people see you, matters.

It matters to others too.

Start giving away truckloads of compliments to others. Confession time: I don't do this enough myself.

Especially with my wife.

Marne is a beautiful woman, both inside and out. She loves Jesus, has the gift of hospitality, cares for others, and is an athlete that loves to have fun in life.

Even though she knows these things, I need to say them more often.

Sidenote: When I write a book, the process always reveals and convicts me of the places I can grow and become more excellent. This area of complimenting others is one of them.

When I deliver a keynote, I pour myself out to inspire, encourage and entertain others. With that goal in mind, it's still great to have people come up and thank me, share wonderful words and give compliments.

Words of affirmation.

You and I need to remember that everyone else desires those positive reminders. A sincere compliment becomes a rocket booster for someone low on fuel. It's joy from your heart to theirs.

Compliments are a gift.

Always and forever.

Always and forever compliment others and count your blessings.

What a great replacement, instead of comparison and complaining we move our thoughts, words and actions to compliments and counting blessings. That movement is the driving force behind your
influential leadership to create impactful results.

Never, ever, ever complain and compare, yet always and forever compliment and count your blessings.

Always and forever compliment others and count your blessings.

Two completely different approaches to life.

A choice you get to make to live every day like a Saturday.

Combine our never, ever, ever and always and forever with

living in the moment, the NOW moment, and you can live the most excellent life.

What a great way to live.

Find out how you can make a difference in others' lives, love them well, and make every day a Saturday.

A day of excellence.

Which leads to a life of excellence.

This is the perfect spot for us to wrap up our conversation and the call to excellence.

I leave you with this poem to ponder.

CLOSING COMMENTS

Throughout this journey we have touched on things,
your life, your work, and areas in between...

Oh so many things we know, believe,
even more things we have seen...

We have talked about movies, and sang some songs,
we have spoken about what is right and wrong...

What is of most importance is that we have reimagined life,
to work, to live and to show our light...

What excellence is, ourselves at our best,
lest we forget we need time to rest...

So my friend, come journey with me,
to a place, a time, your destiny...

A quest for the best, of impact and growth,
a triumph of success unlike the world has known...

I pray for you that God will bless,
each day, each moment and your progress...

For life is made of moments, and a pursuit of what you do,
find your opportunity, the world is waiting for you!

-Randy

ACKNOWLEDGEMENTS

This project doesn't happen without the vision and insights God downloaded to me. The entire pursuit of the book was over a year in the making, and I'm thankful for what He has provided to me.

To my team: Marne, Trevor and Eli, thank you for taking my ideas/writings and concepts and helping to turn them into this wonderful book. Appreciate you all and your talent!

To you, the reader: Grateful you spent your time, talent and treasure with me. Can't wait to see what you do to change the world and make it a little more excellent.

ABOUT THE AUTHOR

Randy Fox is on a mission to help leaders and teams transform their professional and personal lives. His vision is to change the world by developing superstar leaders who make a real difference.

Randy is honored to hold the esteemed designation of Certified Speaking Professional with the National Speakers Association and is the author of several impactful books.

Prior to becoming an internationally acclaimed speaker, author, and professional development coach, Randy earned his stripes with 23 years as an NCAA basketball official and 20 years filled with much success (and some failure too) as a corporate operations and sales leader.

Randy and his wife Marne live in Central Florida, where they are very active in their local community. When he's not in the office or traveling for an event, you're likely to find Randy serving in his church, playing pickleball with neighbors, or coaching youth sports.

OPPORTUNITIES TO CONTINUE EXPLORING

THE CALL TO EXCELLENCE

THE KEYNOTE

It's time for impactful results! Inspire your event attendees and propel them into action with Randy's high-energy, interactive keynote experience.

THE COMPANION VIDEO COURSE

Are you hungry for more stories and strategies?
Check out the Video Course, which includes nearly 2 hours

of content from Randy geared to help you deliver impactful results and be fulfilled in your life.

To access the video course, scan this QR code:

THE LEADERSHIP DEVELOPMENT PROGRAM

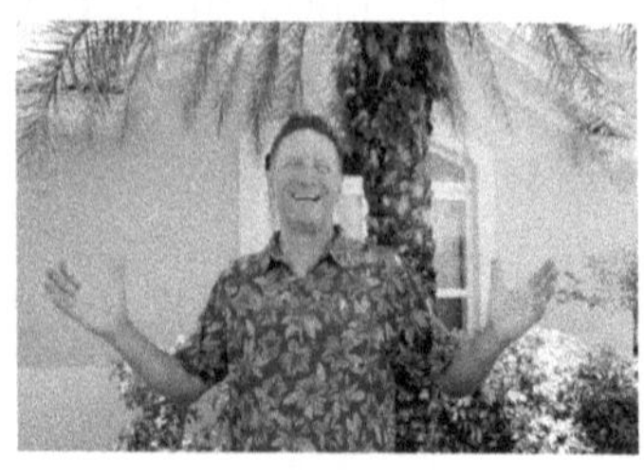

If you're looking for a really deep dive, the Leadership Development Program is made for you! Participants receive personalized professional coaching in this one-year, transformational experience.

To learn more about these opportunities, visit *www.foxpoint.net* or email Trevor from Randy's team at *trevor@foxpoint.net*.

MORE BY RANDY FOX

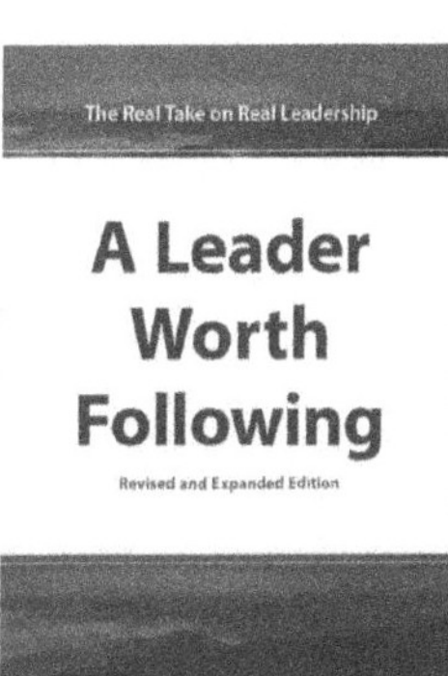

A LEADER WORTH FOLLOWING

Increase Influence. Build Unity. Leave a Legacy. This inspirational read is practical and filled with strategies on being a real leader, one that others willingly follow. Be a leader that changes the world!

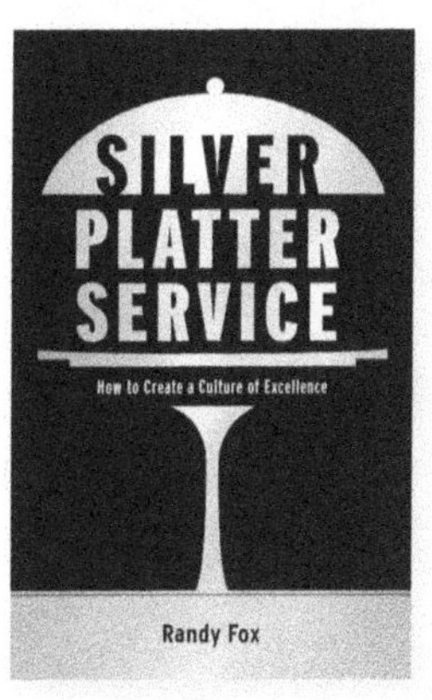

SILVER PLATTER SERVICE

Are you ready to transform the culture of your team? This book is packed with powerful teamwork success stories and actionable strategies to help you create a culture of excellence.

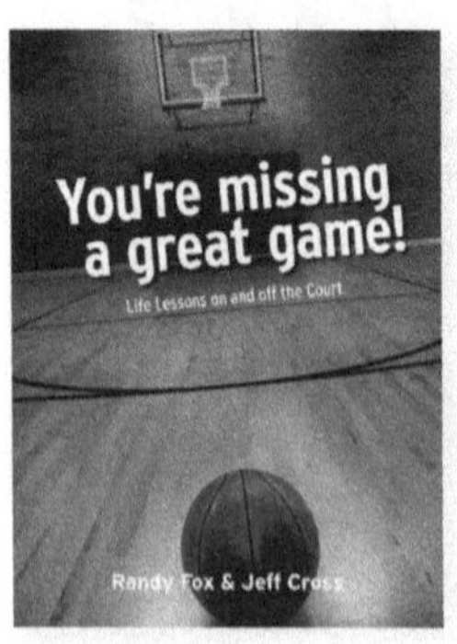

YOU'RE MISSING A GREAT GAME

Randy Fox and Jeff Cross explore invaluable lessons from on and off the court. Learn how to enjoy the great game of life by showing up, playing the game, and discovering the lessons and principles that will help you along the way.

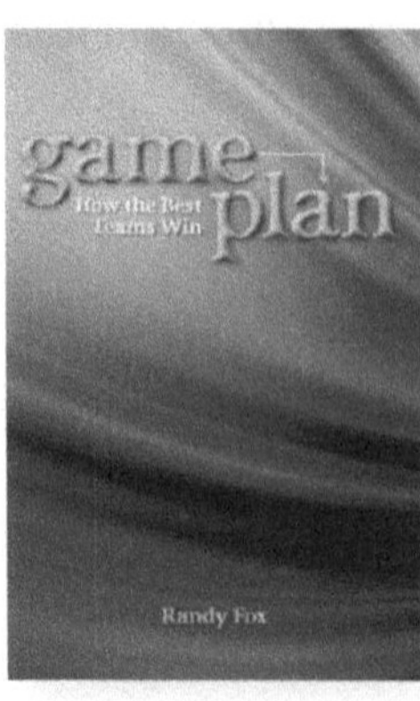

GAME PLAN

Discover the 9 strategies every winning team adapts, implements, and executes to find and sustain their victory!

See the updated list of Randy's books at *www.foxpoint.net/shop*.

www.ingramcontent.com/pod-product-compliance
Lightning Source LLC
Chambersburg PA
CBHW021141090426
42740CB00008B/885

* 9 7 8 0 9 9 1 4 6 6 9 7 9 *